EDUCATION *and*
SOCIAL CHANGE

SOCIOLOGY *and* SOCIAL CHANGE

Series Editor: *Alan* Warde, University of Manchester

EDUCATION *and* SOCIAL CHANGE

Amanda **Coffey**

Open University Press
Buckingham · Philadelphia

Open University Press
Celtic Court
22 Ballmoor
Buckingham
MK 18 1XW

email: enquiries@openup.co.uk
world wide web: www.openup.co.uk

and
325 Chestnut Street
Philadelphia, PA 19106, USA

First Published 2001

A catalogue record of this book is available from the British Library

ISBN   0 335 20068 0 (pb)   0 335 20069 9 (hb)

Library of Congress Cataloging-in-Publication Data
Coffey, Amanda, 1967–
    Education and social change / Amanda Coffey.
        p. cm. – (Sociology and social change)
    Includes bibliographical references and index.
    ISBN 0-335-20069-9 – ISBN 0-335-20068-0 (pbk.)
        1. Educational sociology–Great Britain.   2. Educational change–Great Britain.
        3. Education and state–Great Britain.   I. Title.   II. Series.

LC191.8.G7 C64   2001
306.43'0941–dc21   00-052453

Typeset by Graphicraft Limited, Hong Kong
Printed in Great Britain by Biddles Ltd, Guildford and King's Lynn

To Rhiannon, Jamie, Catrin, Ewan, Jonathan, Alistair, Arran, Nina and Shona and their educational futures

Contents

Series editor's preface

In response to perceived major transformations, social theorists have offered forceful, appealing, but contrasting accounts of the predicament of contemporary western societies with important and widespread ramifications for the analysis of all areas of social life and personal well-being. The speculative and general theses proposed by social theorists must be subjected to evaluation in the light of the best available evidence if they are to serve as guides to understanding and modifying social arrangements. One purpose of sociology, among other social sciences, is to marshal the information necessary to estimate the extent and direction of social change. This series is designed to make such information, and debates about social change, accessible.

The focus of the series is the critical appraisal of general, substantive theories through examination of their applicability to different institutional areas of contemporary societies. Each book introduces key current debates and surveys of existing sociological argument and research about institutional complexes in advanced societies. The integrating theme of the series is the evaluation of the extent of social change, particularly in the last twenty years. Each author offers explicit and extended evaluation of the pace and direction of social change in a chosen area.

Amanda Coffey offers careful and critical reflection on controversial debates and issues in educational policy and educational research during the 1990s. She analyses the ways in which changes in educational policy have affected the experience of education both for students and teachers. Very mindful of inequalities of gender, race and sexuality, she discusses issues that anyone with a concern for education will consider to be important. The book is based on a thorough survey of a wide body of literature in the sociology of education concerning not only institutional change but also methodological and ethical matters entailed in the research process. It makes a distinctive contribution to a field which continues to be responsible for generating considerable political disagreement.

Alan Warde

Acknowledgements

I am grateful to colleagues in the School of Social Sciences, Cardiff University for providing a supportive writing environment. I would especially like to acknowledge Robert Evans, Tom Hall, Trevor Welland, Phil Brown, Ian Welsh, Harry Collins, Paul Atkinson, Sara Delamont and Huw Beynon. I am also grateful to Justin Vaughan and Ros Fane at Open University Press and Alan Warde for their encouragement and patience. Much love and thanks (as always) to Julian. Lastly thank you to my teachers at Countesthorpe College for teaching me the true value of education.

1 Introduction

New rhetorics and repertoires

This book provides a sociological commentary on contemporary educational times. Over the past two decades education has undergone significant transformations, in a context of wider social, economic and policy change. Transformations to education throughout the United Kingdom (UK) have been matched by similar changes elsewhere in the western world. The role of education has been (re)addressed in the light of the cultural and economic transformations of post-industrial societies, as part of an emergent policy repertoire. Shifting relationships between the individual and the state have been matched by rapid social and institutional changes. Postmodern discourses of uncertainty and fragmentation have sat alongside emergent rhetorics of economic efficiency, accountability and effectiveness. Within this changing scene, the role of formal systems of education has been questioned, challenged and realigned. Equally it could be argued that education, broadly conceived, has assumed renewed and increased importance in the quests for economic and social renewal and reconfiguration.

The New Right reforms of education, set in train in the UK following the 1979 election of a Conservative administration, were in part a response to wider concerns (across the political spectrum) about the role of education in post-industrial societies. As a key to economic prosperity, education had been found sadly lacking. By the mid-1970s formal education appeared to have failed in other missions too, such as equality of opportunity and social justice. The 1980s saw education systems ripe for reform, and assuming a central place in the realignment of public services more generally. The rhetorics of choice and diversity were adopted, which in turn altered the organizational, managerial and resource bases of educational provision. These were set into a broader policy framework – which centred the individual and emphasized a strong state. The result was a simultaneous diffusion and concentration of power. Parents were given enhanced choice, and schools given more decision-making and managerial responsibilities, while, at the same time, what was taught, how it was taught and how it was assessed became increasingly centralized.

2   Education *and* social change

The changes that have taken place in education throughout the 1980s and 1990s are now well established, reasonably well documented and have increasingly been subjected to critical analysis. New (national) curricula have been introduced, with attendant pedagogical implications. Enhanced assessment procedures at all levels of compulsory (and indeed non-compulsory) education are now in place. Schools are increasingly subjected to comparative scrutiny, through the publication of league tables of performance and regular inspection by the Office for Standards in Education (Ofsted) (the reports of which are also placed in the public domain). A diversification of school managerial arrangements has been encouraged through the local management of schools and grant maintained status, as well as the introduction of specialist schools and colleges. This diversification squares well with the pursuit of policies designed to create and enhance markets in education; whereby parents have the right to choose schools, and schools must seek ways to attract 'consumers'. Changes have also taken place in other sectors of education. Further and higher education have undergone similar processes of realignment. Teacher education and training has been reorganized, and the Teacher Training Agency established to ensure high standards and foster a regime of accountability. These extensive changes have had profound impacts on the relationship between education and the state and on the working conditions of teachers and learners.

To some extent we have witnessed the emergence of a policy consensus about the role of education. The new Labour administration in the UK, in place since 1997, has not made any significant moves to retract educational policy reforms of the recent decades. If anything a tougher line on issues such as testing and assessment, school (and teacher) inspection and educational management issues has been taken. The market philosophy that enshrines the contemporary educational arena looks relatively safe in these new hands. What has altered, perhaps, is the framing rhetoric that accompanies these policy agendas, with an increased emphasis on notions of community, democracy, citizenship, participation and empowerment, set within the broader context of a learning society. Thus the extension of educational change has been (re)cast to take account of these changing political aspirations. But the direction of change has remained relatively consistent.

While there is a policy consensus, albeit reformulated, there are still tensions between policy imperatives and the lived reality of education. Many aspects of educational change – such as teacher training, new curricula and the (re)definition of knowledge, funding and school management, the new school inspection systems, testing and assessment, parental choice and school selection – remain areas of contention and conflict. Equally, there are areas of education that have remained relatively untouched by recent reforms. For example, it could be argued that equality and social justice issues have remained at the periphery of contemporary educational priorities. Hence significant commentary and critique have accompanied the new educational agendas. These are explored in the course of this volume.

(Re)positioning the sociology of education

The transformations that have taken place in education over recent decades have affected the place of sociology within education, and the sociology of education as an empirical discipline. The new policy repertoires have played a significant part in a detheorizing project. Sociology as a school discipline has been undermined in national curricula, and is no longer a theoretical marker in education, for example in the training of teachers. Educational research agendas have become increasing policy-driven, related more to evaluation than interpretation. This has probably led to a decrease in academics working in the field, certainly those that clearly identify themselves as sociologists of education. It has also meant an ambiguous significance for sociological work on education more generally (see Delamont 2000, for an account of the ambiguous position of sociology of education within the discipline of sociology as a whole).

An alternative perspective would be to stress the rich educational landscape that has resulted from these policy shifts. The changes to educational arenas have provided the opportunities for a remapping of this landscape. Classic sociological questions about the relations between education, economy and society or structural relationships between education and other social 'institutions' have needed to be revisited in the light of reform. At the same time, new areas of research and analysis have been generated – as new structures and processes have been augmented. Contemporary sociology of education must also be placed within broader disciplinary contexts and social movements. The challenges of postmodernism, and alternative perspectives offered by social movements such as anti-racism, feminism and queer studies, have provided new frameworks of analysis, including a reformulated politics of identity and cultural difference. These have established new research agendas and generated new questions for the sociology of education, as Brown *et al.* (1997: 13) note:

> Whereas the sociology of education was previously dominated by issues of access, selection and equality of opportunity, issues of knowledge, pedagogy and the politics of difference have assumed far greater significance in the study of education as a site of struggle. This reflects broader debates within the social sciences about postmodernism and the cultural politics of difference.

In many ways the sociology of education has undergone transformations of its own, paralleling the changes that have taken place in its research sites. It is perhaps useful to characterize these transformations in terms of emergent strands. First, without doubt there is now a substantial amount of policy sociology being undertaken in educational arenas. However, given the relatively weak position of the sociology of education within the discipline more generally, and the ways in which sociology has systematically been linked to radical, subversive or soft perspectives, the suffusion of sociological analyses, strategies and perspectives are often played down. Second, sociologists of education have been increasingly concerned with educational discourses, experiences and identities. That is concerned with mapping and understanding the ways in which discourse shapes and is shaped by multiple educational realities. This draws on critical perspectives and qualitative research strategies, and has focused on articulating the gendered, sexualized, racialized and biographical contexts of teaching and learning. Third, there has been a movement towards a new political arithmetic model (Brown *et al.* 1997), which reformulates some of the classic sociological relations of class, family (in)equality and education. This has sought to rise to the challenge of charting the educational landscape, in socially accountable ways. This responds to some of the critiques of the postmodern position and re-establishes the need for quantifiable data, while recognizing that this must be placed in the context of mapping the *process* as well as the *outcomes* of education. As one of the major institutions of modern society, education has enjoyed a resurrection as vital agent of social change and cultural reproduction (or interruption). As a discipline, sociology is primarily concerned with documenting, explaining and understanding social processes and social change. Hence sociology has a major role to play in making sense of contemporary educational transformations, and relating these to wider processes of social and cultural change.

Aims and scope of the book

Education and Social Change has been written against this backdrop of changing educational times, social and economic transformations and attendant shifts in the sociology of education. The book aims to explore the contexts and policies that have shaped educational change over recent decades, through an engagement with sociological commentary and critical perspectives. The book reflects three levels of transformation.

1   Changing educational landscape(s)

Over the course of the book, many of the educational reforms that have occurred over the last twenty years or so are documented and subjected to critical scrutiny. To focus the discussion, school reforms in the UK (and specifically England and Wales) are used as the main descriptive framework. Cross-references are made to other educational sectors, to illustrate the pervasiveness of the policy climate. Comparative materials from Europe, Australia, New Zealand and North America are also drawn upon, as part of a broader locationary process. A main aim of the text is to demonstrate that the landscape of state education has undergone significant change, and that this has consequences for institutions, professionals, social groups and individuals, as well as for the focus of sociological research. A theme running through the book is an examination of the extent to which these shifts have fundamentally altered the processes, outcomes and lived realities of schooling. Arguably there has been a good deal of educational continuity in the face of change. While there is much that is new – curricula, markets, assessment and inspection procedures, teacher training guidelines and practices, a new promotional culture and recast educational providers and consumers – there are still gendered teacher careers, everyday experiences of the classroom teacher at the 'chalk face', differential educational performances and outcomes, school stratifications, and a range of identities and biographies being crafted and (re)produced with/in educational settings. Hence with change comes continuity. The balance between the two is a theme running through the chapters.

2 Social, cultural, economic and policy transformations

Education provides a solid case study from which to observe and make sense of wider shifts in social, cultural and economic life. Education systems have been repositioned as central to the processes of cultural reproduction and economic regeneration. Shifting labour market needs, the move to credentialism and notions of the learning society have played important roles in rethinking the aims and outcomes of education. At the same time cultural arenas and social institutions have been recast in the light of both economic factors and contemporary social movements. Conceptualizations of the family, sexuality, contemporary racisms, the state, the city, leisure spaces and workplaces have been challenged and reformulated – within and beyond educational arenas. Education policy formations should, therefore, be viewed as both specific to the recasting of a particular institution and set of social processes and indicative of more general and widespread policy cultural, economic and policy agendas. The connection between the specific and the general provides one of the main elements running through the book.

3 New directions for the sociology of education

Sociological work on education has also undergone transformations, which are documented and explored in the course of the book. Social science generally, and sociology in particular, has benefited from (and been challenged by) the perspectives and theorizing offered by a range of new social movements, for example postmodernism, post-structuralist feminism, post-colonialism and anti-racism. These have permeated through to the sociology of education, which has benefited from these new theoretical frameworks and 'ways of seeing'. The emergent policy agendas have provided whole new research agendas, as well as new contexts for exploring long-standing sociological concerns. So alongside critical commentary on the range of policy measures has come re-examination of issues such as educational outcomes, social and educational stratification, equality and social justice, knowledge, pedagogy and educational processes. Arguably policy transformation has given rise to a renewed, sociologically informed research effort (although this kind of policy research is often not self-defined as sociological). Equally there has been increasing funding opportunities for policy-informed educational research. Hence sociological work on education has had to adapt, at least in part, in order to survive.

The last two decades have also witnessed methodological developments and innovations in social science research. These have informed, challenged and changed the ways in which research is undertaken and represented, not least in educational studies. These have partly come about as a response to postmodern, feminist and other critiques of social science research, and have set about rethinking the processes, practices, relationships and outcomes of research endeavours. Educational research has been relatively slow to respond to the new opportunities put forward by such critiques, and it would be wrong to over-emphasize the impact of such articulations on the sociology of education in particular. Equally it would be misguided to argue that postmodern discourse and practices have passed by unnoticed. The biographical or narrative turn has had an important impact on the ways in which educational experiences, processes and policies are researched and understood. Similarly those working within educational/sociological research have addressed issues of representation, and new representational modes have been tried. Sociological work in the field of education has also been the subject of recent (and ongoing) methodological critique and debate of its own. This adds a further dimension to understanding the transformations that have occurred within the subdiscipline.

Education and Social Change draws on a range of contemporary examples, and engages with a range of literature in order to explore these different layers of transformation. Themes which run throughout the book include

- The dynamic relationship between state, institution and individual; examining the shifting boundaries, changes and continuities in the context of educational, economic and social transformation.
- The notion of the educational trajectory or career; understanding the differential outcomes and pathways of educational actors and institutions (learners, teachers, schools) and the ways in which these are reproduced and/or interrupted in new educational times.
- Educational biographies and the politics of identity; the connections between educational experiences and the (re)construction of identities in contemporary society. This engages with contemporary understandings of multiple (fragmented) identities, and recognizes the importance of biographizing (and representing) the social.

Organization of the book

The chapters of the book are thematically organized, to reflect major areas of contemporary educational policy, practice and sociological research. The first three chapters that follow this introduction are all concerned with changes to the educational policy arena, and the ways in which these have impacted on processes, practices and experiences. Chapter 2 addresses the auditing of education and particularly focuses attention on the enhanced evaluation and inspection of schools and teachers (and students, families and communities). It highlights the changes that have taken place to these inspection processes, and the ways in which these have led to a new culture of surveillance within educational arenas. The definition and reality of school failure is examined. Chapter 3 explores the concept and realities of marketization in relation to recent educational reforms, in particular considering how the quasi-marketing of schools has operated in practice. This includes an examination of issues such as parental choice (and empowerment), marketing strategies and the promotional culture. Chapter 4 examines contemporary understandings (and questionings) of educational knowledge, contextualized by the definition and implementation of national curricula. This relates a particular policy formulation to wider sociological questions of the legitimation and certification of particular versions of knowledge. The chapter adopts a broad understanding of what counts as knowledge, in order to explore relationships between school and knowledge (re)production.

The book then turns to a consideration of the experiences and outcomes of educational processes, through an exploration of educational trajectories and biographies. Chapter 5 engages with the biographical or narrative turn in educational research, in order to explore processes of identity (re)construction within a framework of the politics of cultural difference. The lives and experiences of teachers and students are explored in this context, through selected examples of educational identity (or biographical) work. Chapter 6 addresses recurrent themes of the sociology of education, namely outcomes and (in)equality. The chapter specifically locates educational outcomes to economic and social transformations. It revisits issues of inequality and social justice, and engages with contemporary research and policy debates about the role of education in post-industrial society. Contemporary debates about educational achievement are also addressed here. Teachers, and the work that they do, form the focus of Chapter 7. While the experiences and biographies of teachers are discussed throughout the book, it also seems appropriate and timely to consider transformations (and continuities) to the teacher's work and the teaching profession as separate topics. Teachers are critical to policy implementation and to the day-to-day operation of educational life. This chapter hence explores contemporary teaching realities in the light of policy transformation and educational continuities.

The final substantial chapter of the book moves the focus to methodological concerns and research praxis within the sociology of education. I have chosen to include such a chapter in order to document the transformations that have taken place, and are still taking place in social research and the ways in which these relate to educational research. Sociological work on education has been at the centre of recent methodological controversy, as well as playing a part in reshaping the discipline. This parallels the transformations taking place in education and the ways in which these relate to social, economic and policy shifts. The chapter explores some of the recent methodological debates that have occurred within the subdiscipline, and also considers wider criticisms of educational research. This chapter also engages with new methodological innovation, especially in the area of representation.

While *Education and Social Change* has been written as a coherent text, its internal organization means that individual chapters can be read on a stand-alone basis. This, together with an aim of making the text accessible to a wide readership, means that there is a degree of repetition between chapters. This does, however, enable links to be drawn between issues, debates, empirical examples and further reading.

2 Auditing education

Introduction

This chapter explores some of the ways in which surveillance and audit have played an increasingly important role in contemporary educational discourse. Schools, alongside other institutions concerned with educational provision, have become the subject of enhanced scrutiny, as attention has increasingly focused on standards, accountability and effectiveness. This trend is visible across the educational spectrum, including further and higher education sectors who have been forced to address the quality of education they provide, and the ways in which institutions discharge their responsibilities over the standards of their awards (Broadfoot 1998; QAA 1999). Hence while this chapter specifically focuses on the process, experiences and consequences of 'audit' in the school sector, many of the trends and concerns which are illuminated have a wider significance.

The school effectiveness movement, and latterly the school improvement movement, have enjoyed unprecedented recognition over recent decades, as attention has increasingly turned to debates about standards, accountability and effectiveness in education (Sammons *et al.* 1994; Stolland and Mortimore 1995; White and Barber 1997; Gray *et al.* 1999; Morley and Rassool 1999; Teddlie and Reynolds 1999). Calls for greater accountability and measurable school improvement have led to the increased scrutiny of education as a whole, and of schools in particular. These trends can usefully be located within what has been termed a new educational orthodoxy of 'outcomes rhetoric' (Smyth and Dow 1998: 292). Commenting particularly on the Australian context, though equally applicable to the situation in the United Kingdom, Smyth and Dow (1998: 292) liken educational outcomes rhetoric to

> the full sized wood and canvas mock-ups of armoured tanks used in warfare. When the educational auditors fly over schools, they will see row upon row of fierce looking outcomes neatly nested in action plans and teachers' classroom plans, all pointed pugnaciously at groups to be controlled within the school.

There are contrastive trends at work in the strengthening of the argument for desirable and, importantly, measurable educational outcomes. The
seemingly upward trends in some measures of educational success (headline
statistics of improving national examination performance, for example)
have given rise to increased expectations, competitively played out in, for
instance, the annual publication of public examination results. At the same
time there remain long-standing concerns about declining standards, and in
particular the ability of the educational system to respond to the shifting
demands of the economy and the labour market (Brown 1997; Smyth and
Dow 1998). Of course, the present discourse of declining educational standards in the UK stretches back to the Black papers of the 1960s and Callaghan's
now infamous Ruskin College speech (see Wright 1983). The New Right's
'discourse of derision' of education systems (see Ball 1990; also Berliner and
Biddle 1995) was a recurring political theme of the 1980s and 1990s, as were
the attendant moral panics about the effectiveness (or failure) of schools and
teachers to ensure educational success for all (or some) of its consumers (see
Chapter 6). New Labour's educational agenda in Britain has done nothing to
curb concerns about standards. Indeed, it could readily be argued that educational standards, school (and teacher) failure, and school improvement have
been more firmly placed on the political agenda since the election of the
Labour government in 1997 (see Hatcher and Jones 1996 for a summary of
New Labour's educational agenda on which they fought the general election). The present administration have been particular vigorous, for example,
in the identification of schools deemed to be failing (DfEE 1997).

Recurrent debates over the achievements, outcomes and roles of schools
help to locate particular concerns over educational standards, and the effectiveness of schools to ensure and improve them. The parameters of these
debates have been marked by various panics over failure (of pupils, teachers,
schools) and the incorporation of various comparative criteria, for example
unfavourable comparisons between UK school pupils and their peers in Europe, and historical comparative measures between 'then' and 'now'. At one
and the same time government is celebrating the raising of examination
performances, while questioning the lowering of standards, and simultaneously arguing that pupils are leaving school without the 'right' skills, competencies and knowledges to function in a changing labour market. Concerns
over teacher training and education, and teacher incompetence in the classroom, have been paralleled by perceived poor student behaviour (made
visible, for example, through selectively increased rates of both truancy
and exclusion). More recently attention has focused on the apparent failure of
schools to engage with, and ensure the educational success of, boys (Epstein
et al. 1998; Raphael Reed 1999). 'Schools failing boys' is actually the latest in
a long litany of 'worries' about school effectiveness and educational standards. These contemporary worries have consolidated the desire (and some
would argue the need) to assess and improve school performance. This has
given rise to an increased host of measures which are designed to:

• inspect and survey schools to 'measure' educational standards and performances;

- encourage schools and teachers to self-review and seek ways of ensuring enhanced accountability and improvement;
- bring about changes in the overall fortunes of schools – providing 'carrots and sticks' to halt school failure and increase tangible success.

These measures have in common the capacity for surveillance, and comparison between and within schools. They have included an increased emphasis on normative pupil assessment at all educational levels (including primary schooling); the public scrutiny of assessment and examination performance through annual publications of 'league tables' of results; and the regular inspection of schools, the results of which are also placed in the public domain. All of these provide opportunities for politicians and 'consumers' to undertake comparative work, and to identify schools which are deemed to be 'failing' – in terms of (some combination of) accountability, management, teacher effectiveness, pupil behaviour, and examination performance.

The trends toward an overt concern with educational standards, and attendant measures designed to address such 'worries', cannot and should not be viewed in isolation from the broader picture. Terms such as accountability, effectiveness, efficiency and quality are familiar industrial metaphors now readily applied to the range of public services. The increased marketization of public services in general has brought new and enforced regimes of surveillance and monitoring, and a concern with ensuring 'value for money'. The commodification of the educational market place (see Chapter 3) has brought with it an increased remit to 'audit' the processes and outcomes of education. And these are mixed blessings. Schools can successfully 'play the game' as a mechanism of ensuring buoyant student numbers, and the funding that follows, while the identification of failing schools has enormous consequences for teachers, pupils, parents and communities. The concern with measurable outcomes of education can set about raising 'academic' standards, but at the expense of other educational concerns, such as social justice issues (although, as Hargreaves and Moore (2000: 27) argue, outcomes-based education can also foster other more progressive possibilities, such as 'stronger collegiality among teachers, and democratic inclusion of pupils and parents in the teaching and learning process'). Likewise increasing preoccupations with the professional accountability of teachers can be perceived in different and contrastive ways. Concerns over accountability have led to the increased auditing of the teacher's role, and the consequent identification of 'good' and 'bad' teachers. This has placed (in some cases insurmountable) pressures on teachers, both individually and collectively. Equally, the teacher discourse of professionalism can bring with it a renewed commitment to collective autonomy and regulation, self-examination and self-review. Hence the articulation of measurements such as accountability can be used as a mechanism of ensuring the enhanced professional standing of teachers, although many, including the teacher trade unions, have not seen it in this light, perhaps with good reason.

This chapter draws on this changing culture of education – toward increasing auditability and a concern with standards – in order to examine the discourses of success and failure in education and schools. In engaging with the outcomes rhetoric, the chapter explores some of the processes and potential consequences of these contemporary educational discourses. The following section considers the ways in which schools and teachers are now routinely assessed and compared, and examines the lived reality of these undertakings. The chapter then goes on to explore the phenomenon of the 'failing school', and the impact of increased surveillance and calls toward effectiveness and accountability on the everyday experiences of education.

The surveillance of schools and inspection of teachers

While schools, and indeed teachers, have always been subjected to some level of normative inspection procedure, the 1990s saw more stringent and regulated mechanisms emerge. In England and Wales, the Office for Standards in Education (Ofsted) set up a new system of school inspection in 1992, as a direct result of the Education (Schools) Act of the same year. This was an ambitious revamp of pre-existing inspection mechanisms (a mixture of Her Majesty's Inspectorate (HMI) and local education authority inspection), and aimed to put in place a standardized, regular (four-yearly) primary and secondary school inspection system. This new system was also to be (notionally) independent. Inspection teams were to be accredited by Ofsted, and would contain a mixture of educational professionals and lay members, trained prior to inspection. School inspections would be carried out according to a declared framework of measurable criteria, and would be formulated to incorporate all aspects of the school. The scheme effectively replaced all of the existing systems of 'advice-based' inspection, and introduced a unified, centralized system of school inspection and surveillance. In doing so the emphasis of 'school inspection' shifted from an implicit one of advice and support to an explicit one of assessment and measurement of the quality of the school – in terms of procedures, management, standards and outcomes (Clegg and Billington 1994; Webb *et al.* 1998).

Ofsted inspectors are charged with assessing the standards of achievement and the quality of education provided in individual schools, and across local education authorities. They have a number of mechanisms to hand with which to undertake this task. Examination and assessment performance league tables provide explicit measurement criteria, as do routinely recorded data on levels of attendance, absence, exclusion and truancy. Evidence of the efficient management of resources can also be readily gathered, including details of financial controls and mechanisms that are in place, and how these are implemented at the local and school levels. Teacher development and appraisal procedures can also be inspected and monitored. All of these data are able to contribute to a substantial 'paper' audit of the school, and involve considerable documentary preparation by the school in advance of an Ofsted visitation, which also consists of direct observation of the school environment, teachers, pupils and classrooms. These serve as mechanisms for assessing the quality of teaching provision, and the role of the school in the academic and social development of pupils. Ofsted has no official advisory role, the emphasis being on inspection rather than advice. However, the commitment it made in 1994 to the motto 'improvement through inspection' carries the implicit idea that the process of inspection can help schools to identify targets, and to improve, as Webb *et al.* (1998: 541) note:

> Each school has to produce an 'action plan' following an inspection to indicate the procedures by which it intends to implement recommendations arising from the inspection. Such action plans take on a special significance in those schools that have been judged to be 'failing' and which are then subject to a follow up inspection to monitor their implementation.

The model of school inspection operationalized through this Ofsted system, and maintained through the change of government administration in 1997, articulates particular understandings of educational measurement. These carry with them specific interpretations of educational (school) success, failure and improvements, and exacerbate tensions between inspection and the everyday realities and roles of the school. A number of specific points can be made with regard to this.

1 The framework of inspection leads to the development and support of technical and auditable criteria (what Smyth and Dow (1998) refer to as a form of technical rationality). Measurable factors are given precedence over less tangible or tacit factors, and to some extent the work of the teacher is compartmentalized and routinized. This is perhaps an inevitable consequence of any system of explicit measurement and comparison. However, it is worth noting that the Ofsted process concentrates weight on 'independent' judgement of measurable criteria, rather than a more general (self-) evaluation of and by the school. The notion of external accountability lends itself to the enhanced provision of 'written policies, systems and procedures' (Webb *et al.* 1998: 553), rather than the development of more general school values and activities. That is not to say that one does not enhance the other (see Hargreaves and Moore 2000).

2 The favoured model of teaching and learning implicitly supported by Ofsted is a transmissional one 'in which information is passed to students and a student is seen as developing in terms of attainment and progress through the manifest technical skills of the teacher' (Woods and Jeffrey 1998: 548). Teachers are central to this model of inspection, both as managers of the school and as classroom practitioners. Indeed, during the 1990s the chief inspector of schools for England placed increasing amounts of emphasis on the inspection of classroom teaching, and the explicit correlation between raising standards and the need to identify, and where possible remove 'failing' teachers (Ofsted 1995, 1996).

3 The adopted model of inspection exacerbates potential tensions between measuring quality and standards *and* measuring 'value-added' impacts of a school. While researchers working within the traditions of school effectiveness and social improvement (see Teddlie and Reynolds 1999) have

each identified value-added criteria in assessing the effectiveness of a school, such criteria are difficult to square alongside the explicit auditing function of formal school inspection. While inspectors are charged with taking into account, where possible, value-added measures and how far the school contributes to the academic and pastoral progress of its pupils, using such techniques as a formal way of assessing and comparing schools remains difficult to operationalize under the present standards-driven regime. The systematic collection of longitudinal data which could measure value-addedness is far from complete, although the new early 'testing' of primary school children through the standard assessment tests that have been intro-duced may make this more possible in future. There are other difficulties in trying to assess the value-added potential of the school, some of which have been identified by the Organization for Economic Cooperation and Development (OECD) (1995). For example the danger of legitimizing lower attainment standards for pupils from lower socio-economic backgrounds; the potential for the majority of schools to 'average out' under value-added analysis with any differences being at the extremes; and the mean-ingfulness of value-added debates in the face of marketization and school choice (see Chapter 3). Indeed, under a regime of school choice, parents may increasingly opt for less 'value-added' schools over those with difficult and varied pupil intakes (and hence more value-added potential!). Never-theless the debates over value-addedness of schooling are important ones, significantly so where schools may be deemed to be failing according to the inspection-led measurable criteria but still maintain they are providing their pupils with meaningful educational experiences.

4 An implication of the present inspection regimes is a tight regulatory and surveillance machinery. This repositions the relationship between the school and the state, and exacerbates tensions between the local and the central. The tensions between centralization and decentralization are especially apparent under these new auditing regimes, as schools are now expected to demonstrate their adherence to indicators and criteria over which they have little control. As Hexhall and Mahony (1998: 137–8) have suggested:

> League tables, quality indicators, appraisal procedures, profiling and differentially rewarding quality teachers are all devices for individualis-ing institutional or personal judgements of effectiveness, whether of schools . . . or specific teachers. Such attributions of localised responsib-ility are seen as powerful methods for 'ratching up standards' . . . such measures occur in a policy context in which the room for manoeuvre is highly constrained.

The auditing of schooling, epitomized by the surveillance and inspection mechanisms of Ofsted, is indicative of trends visible across different educa-tional sectors and in international contexts. Hexhall and Mahony (1998) identify the setting up of the Teacher Training Agency (TTA) in England in 1994 as to some extent mirroring the processes occurring at the school level. The TTA is charged with improving the quality of teaching and raising standards in teacher training and education. The range of activities and initiatives recently or currently being introduced by the TTA, such as a national curriculum for teacher education, national professional standards and qualifications, and the (re)certification of head teachers, are concerned with *both* increasing the effectiveness of teachers *and* restructuring the profession in terms of power, responsibility and accountability. The occupational lives of teachers are increasingly coordinated, defined and regulated. In higher and further education, similar trends are apparent. For example, the continuation audit (QAA 1998), disciplinary benchmarking and the proposed accreditation of academic faculty through the newly formed Institute of Learning and Teaching are indicative of measures designed to increase accountability and auditability in higher education. International comparison also reveals that these moves toward increased educational surveillance are not confined to the United Kingdom. As the OECD have identified (1995), the performance of education systems, schools and staff is a growing concern across Europe, as well as in North America, Scandinavia and New Zealand (see Thrupp 1999). And as Mahony (1997) has noted, the recasting of teacher education in the UK within a discourse of educational effectiveness is part of an international trend towards a new public management regime.

These processes of transformation in the auditing, measuring and surveillance of education have had profound effects on schools and teachers, who have had to take on board these processes as part of their everyday lives. At best preparing for an Ofsted inspection involves schools and teachers in a substantial amount of preparatory work, demanding time, energy, effort and resources (Campbell and Neill 1994; Webb and Vulliamy 1996; Webb *et al.* 1998). This is particularly salutary when it is recognized that the relationships between preparing for an inspection, the inspection process itself, and any fundamental and long-standing changes in classroom practice are rather tenuous (Webb *et al.* 1998; but see also Hargreaves and Moore 2000 who argue that this does not have to be the case). At worst, school inspection can have far-reaching (and, indeed, shattering) consequences for individual schools and individual teachers. Aside from the tremendous amount of resources demanded as part of the inspection process, a possible outcome of these explicit surveillance mechanisms is the identification of teachers and schools deemed to be failing. In these cases individual teachers may be forced to leave the school (and indeed the teaching profession), schools can receive unwarranted public, political and media attention, school management personnel may be forcibly changed, and as a last resort schools may be faced with closure.

Woods and Jeffrey (1998) have documented how the lives and work of teachers have become increasingly colonized by these processes of inspection and surveillance. Their research was conducted among a sample of six primary schools, all of which underwent their first inspection during 1995–97. The project included participant observation of the inspection process and qualitative interviews with teachers and inspectors. Along with other commentators, Woods and Jeffrey noted the large amount of required documentation and increased workloads that have inevitably accompanied inspection preparation, and identified ways in which teachers have been forced to adopt a variety of coping strategies to deal with these additional demands (see also

Campbell and Neill 1994; Webb *et al.* 1998; Jeffrey 1999). They document the ways in which school inspectors *as well as* teachers 'avail themselves of a range of discourses in negotiating personal ways through structural constraints' (Woods and Jeffrey 1998: 547). Contrastive discourses of the new regimes of inspection and classroom teaching are identified, in a consideration of the ways in which teachers and inspectors manage the everyday context of school inspection. In interpreting the discourses of school inspection, inspectors are identified by Woods and Jeffrey as having a considerable degree of agency, enabling them to negotiate a way through tensions by interpretation and adaptation. Ofsted inspectors bring to their inspection role other selves – they may, for example, have been teachers or educationalists prior to becoming inspectors. Hence they are often able to develop a middle discourse incorporating the frameworks of inspection with some understanding of teaching realities, thus resolving 'contradictions between the technicism of the Ofsted model and their own personal values' (Woods and Jeffrey 1998: 549). However, as Woods and Jeffrey note, teachers at the sharp end of inspection often do not pick up this recast discourse. They may experience value conflict, colonization and deprofessionalization during the inspection process. Teachers are often faced with 'staging a performance' for the purposes of inspection, as a full-time class teacher and deputy head of a primary school acknowledged in research conducted by Webb *et al.* (1998: 547):

> She described her approach to the week's teaching as differing fundamentally from how she usually worked with the children . . . She was 'artificially prepared' because she had a folder for each lesson in which she kept her plan, lesson notes and activity sheets. When the lesson was over she put it back in the store cupboard and took out the one for the next lesson . . . The adverse effects that a poor report can have on individuals and schools encourages teachers to work in ways during an inspection that would neither be viable nor possible to maintain over a longer time span . . . also it seems teachers gain little from the process apart from finding out how well they can operate under duress.

This highlights the ways in which teachers simultaneously distance and engage themselves in the school inspection process, maintaining the self and the everyday reality of the classroom while satisfying corporate pressures and demonstrating high levels of commitment to work. It is not at all clear whether the process of inspection has any positive impacts on the school and the lives of teachers. A successful inspection report/outcome and any consequent positive publicity may be helpful in recruitment and staff morale, and there is some evidence of curriculum developments and practice improvements, or at least their potential (Hargreaves and Moore 2000). But as Webb *et al.* (1998: 552) note, 'when identifying school improvement gains resulting from inspections, the costs to individual teachers and the cumulative impact on schools must also be recognised'. There is little evidence of the inspection process encouraging professional dialogue (Southworth and Fielding 1994) or self-evaluation (Webb *et al.* 1998), and observers have commented that, with the exception of a small number of 'at risk schools', the inspection process is not a significant learning experience (Wilcox and

Gray 1998). The next section of this chapter explores this issue further, by examining one particular outcome of the enhanced inspection and surveillance of schools – the identification of the failing school.

The phenomenon of the failing school

The Office for Standards in Education has been accused of developing an especially harsh approach to the pursuit of educational standards (David 1999). A key aspect of their approach has been the public identification of schools deemed to be failing to meet and maintain educational standards. Public identification of failing schools was justified by the former Chief Inspector of Schools for England (Chris Woodhead) as part of a process of ensuring that honest reports are available to parents about schools, and as a mechanism for encouraging school improvement. However, as Tomlinson (1997, 1998) has argued, the failing schools movement of the 1990s can be seen as the antipathy of the effective schools movement. School effectiveness studies have conventionally been concerned with identifying characteristics of effective schools, and sharing them with practitioners as a means of encouraging good practice (Sammons *et al.* 1994). The 1990s saw these general principles reconceptualized as a political tool, designed to highlight and show school failure and its consequences. The identification and denigration of failing schools as a political tool has been maintained through the shift from Conservative to Labour government in the UK. Indeed, the transition to and consolidation of the new Labour administration has, if anything, increased the concern with educational standards, thus re-emphasizing the process of identifying and publicly naming schools considered to be failing to meet those standards. This heightened impetus to use school inspection as a way of highlighting school failure is not confined to the United Kingdom. Similar processes and trends are evident for example in Europe, North America and New Zealand (see OECD 1995; Thrupp 1999).

The failing schools movement, as a product of 1980s and 1990s legislation, is designed to identify schools with low levels of achievement and poor performance, and put in place action plans for improvement (see Ofsted 1994, 1997). At best failing schools are deemed to be in need of special measures (DoE 1993), in order to improve. At worst the management of the failing school is taken out of the hands of local authorities and/or the local management teams of schools, and placed in the hands of centrally appointed bodies (which may include private sector or voluntary sector consortia) and individuals (so-called 'superheads'). At the extreme a failing school can be closed down, as either a temporary or permanent measure. How failure is defined is directly related to the framework of inspection incorporated into the auditing and surveillance regimes of schools, in train since the late 1980s, and manifested under the auspices of Ofsted. Criteria for failure therefore include a mixture of explicit, measurable factors, and less discernible, more indeterminate variables. Hence measurements such as poor comparative examination performance, high levels of truancy and/or exclusion and high comparative staff turnover/absences are judged alongside other factors – such as teaching deemed unsatisfactory (through direct observation), high staff demoralization, inefficient use of resources, evidence of a loss of confidence in senior staff, poor provision of moral, social, spiritual and cultural guidance and high levels of pupil disruption. The explicit, public 'naming and shaming' of failing schools (or local authorities or head teachers or governors or teachers or pupils) is a particularly harsh consequence of this process. Schools identified as failing through the Ofsted procedures are revealed through publication of the inspection report, and consequent political statements and media attention.

This public demonization of schools in England and Wales began in the early 1990s, but as has already been noted it has shown no sign of abating with the change in central administration. School failure was a key issue of the 1997 general election campaign. The Labour government has continued the process of naming failing schools, putting in place special measures and superheads, and imposing new management regimes (and even closure) on those schools who do not respond to heightened pressures to improve. The announcement in November 1999 by the Secretary of State for Education of the appointment of an independent body to take over the responsibilities of a whole local education authority deemed to be failing suggests that the Labour government has been keen to extend and consolidate this process. The resignations of a number of so-called superheads, some only a year into their job and put in place by the Labour government, have further raised the public and media profile of failing schools. Some of these new head teachers had been in position for only a few months and the evidence that they had managed to 'turn the school around' is at best sketchy. Supporters of the failing schools, and related special measures, legislation have been keen to stress its relative success. It has been argued that while some schools have been closed as a result, these are a relatively small percentage of all those subjected to the process. Most failing schools have been revived by special measures. However it is fair to say that this position is contested. Other commentators have pointed to the increased surveillance that the failing schools process has led to, and the mixed outcomes that have resulted (Slee, Weiner with Tomlinson 1998; Tomlinson 1998; David 1999).

The failing schools movement is an overt manifestation of the more general frameworks of inspection evident in education over recent decades. As such it provides a particularly intense example of more general processes. For example, the concern with measuring standards has led to the increased surveillance of all, but especially failing, schools. Tomlinson's account of the inspection procedures and consequent identification of Hackney Downs school in East London as a failing school (Tomlinson 1997 and 1998) highlights the increased, almost goldfish-bowl-like, surveillance that accompanies these processes. She notes that 'between 1989 and 1995 Hackney Downs must have been the most inspected school in the country' (Tomlinson 1998: 166). She also draws attention to the particular historical context of the failing schools movement. As other commentators have pointed out, school inspection and evaluation have a long history (Slee, Weiner with Tomlinson 1998) and notions of failure are not new (Tomlinson 1997). Indeed, dissatisfaction with the education system and with educational standards is a recurrent and routine pitch. Recent manifestations of this public denigration of schools deemed to be failing can be located within the broader frameworks of a discourse of derision (Ball 1990; Delamont 1999). That is, the identification and public demonization of failing schools form part of a wider contemporary critique of education. This focuses attention on poor teachers, 'subversive' educational theories and progressive pedagogies in assessing what is wrong with education. This discourse, though usually associated with New Right agendas, has a more general resonance through the failing schools movement.

An element of this process is an implicit apportioning of blame. Through the inspection and identification process school failure is individualized, and blame placed firmly at the feet of individual 'failing' teachers and poor local management. Teachers, heads and governors all come under increased scrutiny, although, as David (1999) notes, a knock-on effect is that pupils, parents and communities are also blamed for the failure of the school. Special measures work with this individualized framework, and tend toward the ignoring of wider structural factors. This individualization of both 'problem' and 'solution' has the capacity for divorcing school failure from wider historical, social, economic and political contexts. Naming and eliminating failing teachers (and replacing 'ineffectual' local school management regimes) displaces school failure from political agendas, and results in demonizing schools for wider economic and social problems. Tomlinson (1998: 55) has argued that 'by the 1990s, politicians were targeting individual "bad" schools as responsible for a situation whereby large numbers of young people, especially from urban, disadvantaged areas had few qualifications of the kind that were deemed necessary for a post industrial society'. David (1999) too has highlighted the relationship between the strategy of identifying failing schools and wider processes of social exclusion. On the whole the schools that have been targeted under the failing schools legislation have been 'located in areas defined as social exclusion and characterised by poverty' (David 1999: 221). She argues that one outcome of this social and political context of naming and shaming has been to demoralize not only schools and teachers, but also parents and children:

> Demoralization may not lead to better educated standards either at home or at school, but rather to reinforcing feelings of inadequacy around parenting and childcare. Thus the opposite effect of social inclusion may be achieved and social exclusion reinforced of the very families, parents and children that a strategy aimed at improving educational standards for all was designed for.
>
> (David 1999: 221)

The failing schools legislation must also be located alongside broader educational change, for example the contexts and frameworks of educational marketization, diversification and privatization (Ball 1994). These identification processes can result in the removal of individual 'failing' schools from local education authority control, and the imposition of new management regimes (with voluntary or private sector involvement). The guise of educational standards can mask actual diversification of school management and organizational regimes. A failure label also places additional pressures on schools to establish a favourable and positive promotional culture, deemed necessary for effective participation in school markets (Thrupp 1999).

The comments made by Slee and Weiner on school effectiveness research have resonance for the so-called schools failure movement. Slee and Weiner (with Tomlinson) (1998: 5) argue that the school effectiveness research 'bleaches context from its analytic frame. It is silent on the impact of the national curriculum, the marketization of schooling, the press for selected entry and grant maintained distinctions on the relative performance of schools.' Similar criticisms could easily be levelled at the processes of identifying school failure through an explicit and centrally driven system of inspection and surveillance. It is arguably the case that the naming and shaming of schools is based on data decontextualized from their political, economic and social frameworks. Similarly 'blaming' is individualized, as opposed to being located within policy and structural contexts. It is in this light that authors such as Tomlinson (1997, 1998) and Thrupp (1999) have stressed caution in claiming that the failing schools movement and accompanying special measures have been an overwhelming success in turning schools around. As Thrupp suggests, an overly optimistic view of special measures paints a rather benign view of the intent of policies, and fails to take into account the negative effects of publicly highlighting schools deemed to be failing. The impacts on school reputations, and staff morale, not to mention the reputations and morale of communities, families, parents and children (David 1999), can be considerable. The narratives of schools 'turned around' on the back of being named, and following the introduction of special measures, tend not to dwell on what Slee (1998) terms 'population cleansing' and large injections of funding not previously made available to the school. It is perhaps not surprising that 'standards' rise when more middle-class pupils are 'bussed in' or when schools are 'suddenly' given more money (Thrupp 1999).

This brings us to a further set of issues around questions of equality and social justice. The school failure debate has been relatively silent in addressing these issues, as Slee (1998) among others (for example Thrupp 1999) has noted. (See Ball 1994: 121, who argues a similar case for the marketization of schooling having 'no commitment to social goals of equality or justice embedded within it'.) The cultural politics of identity and failure have been largely absent from school failure discourses. Similarly scant attention has been paid to the consequences of these naming processes for individual pupils, teachers, parents or local communities. Spooner's narrative of the experiences of two 'failing' schools in the North East of England (Spooner 1998) provides some evidence of the impact of the labelling process on the lives of children and teachers. Teachers were demoralized, hurt and angry, and many good teachers left the schools (and indeed the profession) as a result of this process of identification. Spooner argues that 'politicians often forget that each pupil only has one set of school days' (1998: 151), and hence to be told your school is failing and/or closing due to 'failure' has an enormous impact on the education, experiences and futures of children. The political process of failure labelling is, according to Spooner, probably more damaging than any existing practices and ethos of the school. This takes us back to the notion of value-added, and also to more rounded interpretations of the purposes of schooling. Spooner (1998: 151) argues that 'failing schools' are often actually far from failing in the service they offer to those children who most need what the school can and does provide:

> Boys and girls from deprived backgrounds need to get a sense of secur-
> ity from their schools. Those who struggle academically need to have
> the same teachers for years 10 and 11. Above all else they need to
> acquire self respect and the chances of this are always enhanced when
> they have confidence in the school they attend.

In practice, the impacts of this labelling process have mostly been confined to certain kinds of schools in certain kinds of areas, with certain kinds of pupils. Those that have been 'named' tend to be located in inner city areas, with significant socio-economic deprivation, and significant proportions of minority, migrant and second language pupils, as well as high numbers of pupils with special educational needs (Tomlinson 1997, 1998; David 1999; Thrupp 1999). As Tomlinson (1998: 158) notes of the now infamous Hackney Downs school in East London,

> By the 1990's, two thirds of the pupils had some form of special educa-
> tional need, about 70 percent being second language speakers. A high
> proportion of pupils had been taken in after exclusion from other
> schools. By 1995 the buildings pupils were taught in were, almost
> literally, falling down. Yet this was a school in which teachers in post
> were publicly blamed for short changing the pupils.

A problem with the phenomenon of the failing school is that it only really addresses the 'surface' work of success and failure. By individualizing blame, the problem and the solutions, it fails to acknowledge the socio-economic, historical and policy dimensions of school processes, practices and outcomes. It also silences and fails to recognize the racialized, class-specific, gendered and disabilist 'identities' of school failure. This is not to suggest that there are not schools that are failing their pupils, teachers, parents and communities. Indeed it would be a complacent society (and educational system) to claim that all schools are succeeding for everyone. Rather the strategies for identifying failing schools, and attempts to revive them, are superficial in their analyses of what counts as failure. Naming failing schools with a diverse range of pupils, with differentiated needs, in socially deprived areas, does little to recognize the multiple contexts and outcomes of education, and does not necessarily ensure schools become a better place for teachers, learners and the communities they serve. The failing schools movement can be seen as part of a normalizing project; part of an attempt to set a kind of normative standard through which judgement can be cast on the good and the bad (and indeed the ugly). Pathologizing individual schools (and hence teachers, pupils, parents and communities) obstructs serious consideration of the 'poli-tics of identity and difference in schools and the affirmation of the broader educational goals of social justice and democracy' (Slee and Weiner 1998: 6).

Ball (1997) takes up the labelling of schools as bad and good in his analysis of the impacts of various quality assurance procedures on schools and teachers. Through a case study consideration of a school identified as good, Ball reveals the ways in which 'quality' discourses are articulated and manufactured. 'Martineau' school had positioned itself with/in the quality revolution. They had taken on board 'the new managerial discourse of quality' (Ball 1997: 333). Although that was not the only discourse to which the school subscribed, it played a major part in the ethos, management and everyday work of the school. Ball argues that articulating the notion of the 'good school' within the parameters of the official quality discourse is problematic. Quality assurance measures (such as those advocated by Ofsted) which are set up to encourage the formulation of the good school (as contrasted with the bad/failing school) may actually have adverse effects, such as 'the intensification of teachers' work (often on administrative tasks unrelated to the teaching/learning process), a reduction in teacher collegiality, and the production of fabricated indicators and manufactured representations of "the school"' (Ball 1997: 318). This leads Ball (1997: 334) to conclude that (ironically) what makes a school good may also make it bad (and presumably vice versa), as 'what counts as good and bad, of course, rests on what qualities of institutions are valued'. Thus the distinction between bad schools and good schools may actually tell us very little about educational experiences of teachers, pupils and parents, and may tell us more about the capacity of the school to navigate successfully the various quality discourses.

Conclusion

This chapter has sought to contextualize the inspection and evaluation of schools within broader policy frameworks of audit and surveillance. Recent decades have witnessed unprecedented emphasis on standards in education and one manifestation of that has been the imposition of legislative processes through which schools and teachers are called to account. The contemporary outcomes rhetoric of education has resulted in increasing the measures through which educational institutions and educational actors are evaluated, assessed and judged as part of a continual auditing process. This has had significant consequences for the everyday work of schools and teachers who have had to adapt to new regimes of documentation, accountability and auditability. At the same time it remains unclear whether these new regimes have had any positive or long-lasting impact on the quality of education, on educational standards, on educational outcomes or on the lived realities of education for pupils, students and teachers. The next chapter addresses this same set of issues from a different, though related, perspective. It explores the policy shift towards increased marketization, and considers the consequences of this for educational institutions, providers and consumers.

3 Parents, consumers *and* choice

Introduction

The policy shift toward privatization and the free market provision of public services, crystallized by the Thatcher Conservative administrations of the 1980s, has directly impacted upon the UK education system. The Labour administration, elected in 1997, has continued to support and foster a market philosophy advocated during the 1980s and 1990s. However, there has been some change of emphasis, away from individualization and a 'free market' toward a strengthening of the merits of cooperation, diversity, choice and partnership in a market environment. This has often been referred to as a quasi-market, recognizing that the market forces and relations present within education have been mediated by the state. The introduction and support of a quasi-market in education (Le Grand and Bartlett 1993) cast pupils and students as educational clients. More fundamentally, parents have been recast as the consumers of education systems – involved in the educational decision making for, with and on behalf of their children (David *et al.* 1994; Hughes *et al.* 1994; Gewirtz *et al.* 1995; Gorard 1997a). The advent of 'parentocracy' has been marked as a third wave of state education in the United Kingdom: 'where a child's education is increasingly dependent upon the *wealth* and *wishes* of parents, rather than the *ability* and efforts of pupils' (Brown 1997: 393). This follows a first wave that introduced mass elementary schooling, and a second wave that shifted educational ideology toward meritocracy (and away from earlier notions of social ascription). Parentocracy has added a further dimension to the already complex set of relationships between families and educational institutions (David 1993; David *et al.* 1994; Vincent 1996).

The primacy of choice, especially but not exclusively parental choice, is central to the allocation and understanding of contemporary school provision. The 1988 Education Reform Act of England and Wales, and subsequent legislation, introduced and reinforced notions of choice by encouraging a range of different school types to emerge (locally managed, grant maintained, city technology colleges, specialist). This seeming diversification has accompanied other transformations – to open school enrolment, per capita funding, and the placing of performance indicators (league tables) and school inspection reports in the public arena. A discourse of autonomy (for parents and schools) in a framework of deregulation has provided a context for these shifts. One of the underlying themes of these educational transformations has been the conceptualization of rational choice. At the crux of these reforms, and the resultant educational market place, has been the assumption that parents can, and will, make *informed* decisions about choice of school. These decisions will be based on an appraisal of academic standards, and achievements of schools, epitomized by the publication of performance league tables (and thereby leading schools to address their standards and improve their performance). In practice, research has shown that school choice, in the context of a quasi-market and differential decision-making powers, is much more complex than that simple model would imply. Schools have been drawn into adopting a range of explicit and implicit marketing 'strategies' in their quest to meet their target rolls, and attract parents. As schools have increasingly become competitors in a fluid and volatile market place, they have taken seriously the management of their public image, especially that which is presented to parents as consumers. Hence image management has become increasingly prominent in the state education sector (see Gewirtz *et al.* 1995; Smedley 1995; Hesketh and Knight 1998; Maguire *et al.* 1999).

The development of markets in the compulsory state school sector has been matched by similar shifts in further and higher education. Per capita funding, and the introduction of the tuition fee (Dearing 1997), combined with the reduction in student grant support and the loss of entitlement to state benefits, form part of more general reforms of higher education. Dearing argued that government, students and their parents, universities and employers were all stakeholders in the higher education market place, and should contribute to the funding of higher education. The report recommended that students should be encouraged to invest in themselves, and contribute to the costs of the tuition. While government has not adopted the Dearing proposals unreservedly, it has introduced enhanced income contingent loans to replace student maintenance grants and required all students (subject to means testing) to contribute toward tuition fees. Recent and ongoing debates over the funding of higher education, following constitutional devolution in the UK for example, has ensured that tuition fees, and more generally choice of university, remains high on the educational political agenda. Moreover, higher and further education institutions have also had to address the matter of effective marketing strategies. Potential higher education students, and most often their parents, are now 'customers' with needs to be met and the desire to know what they are paying for (Smith *et al.* 1995; Maguire *et al.* 1999).

This chapter considers the interface between providers and consumers in the educational market place. In doing so, it considers the role of markets in education, in realigning educational experiences to the context of wider social change. The chapter addresses the relationships between education markets, educational choices and educational outcomes, and considers the commodification and marketization of the school. The resultant recast relationship between schools and parents is also addressed. Specifically how parents are involved in the decision-making process about school choice is examined, and set within a framework of parental involvement and parental power.

Choice and the educational market place

The 'school choice' reforms of the 1980s and 1990s in England and Wales have been part of a broader period of change to the infrastructure of education. The impacts of these transformations have been twofold and, at least on the surface, contradictory. Increases in state control and centralization have been matched by moves toward local autonomy at school level. The resultant encouragement of an educational market place has allowed parents a degree of choice over schools, and firmly linked school funding to meeting pupil number targets. These changes have altered both the philosophy and practice of state education, asserting increased control over the everyday work of teachers (see Chapter 7), establishing the requirement that schools 'market' themselves, and altering relationships between schools, parents and communities. This phenomenon, of the increased marketization of public (state) schooling, has not been limited to England and Wales. Researchers have commented on similar trends in, for example, Australia (Kenway 1993) and New Zealand (Robertson 1999; Thrupp 1999). The US educational systems also operate through educational markets, although, as Ball (1994) points out, there are differences between those and the UK model (for example US models tend to be stronger on diversification, parental empowerment and social justice commitments, but weaker on choice than the UK model).

The moves towards parental choice (or at least the parental right to express a choice) in England and Wales have been compounded by the local management of schools (LMS) legislation (under the 1993 Education Act). This legislation sought to devolve to schools many of the responsibilities previously held by local education authorities, including making schools more accountable and responsible for their financial management. LMS brought to the schools everyday control over finances and budgets, and consequent decision-making responsibilities (over, for example, organizational and administrative matters, infrastructure, staffing and pupil rolls). On the surface, at least, this has decreased the centralized control of schools, giving heads and school governors much more power over the day-to-day management of their organizations. In turn, local education authorities have assumed a reduced role, exacerbated by a decreased link between school enrolment and LEA-designated catchment areas. Local management of schools was accompanied by two other changes to the ways in which state education in England and Wales was conceived: a policy of open enrolment and a pupil-led funding formula. Schools as providers and stakeholders have become increasingly dependent on pupil rolls for primary funding. Poor levels of enrolment have an immediate fiscal impact on the school. Hence it has become increasingly important for schools to attract 'customers' (pupils and, more importantly, their parents) in order to secure a healthy level of enrolment. This has fostered new relationships between schools, pupils and parents

(Power *et al.* 1998b; Reay 1998; David 1999). In an era, at least in theory, of open enrolment, schools must seek to attract, and parents choose to send, pupils from outside the local 'catchment' area of the school. In practice there is empirical evidence to suggest that school choice is related to social class differentials, with middle-class parents more able and more likely to exercise choice 'outside' local catchment areas.

> In an education market (a) the strategic processes of choice systematically disadvantage working class families and (b) the link between choices and resources (via per capita funding) disadvantages working class schools and communities (ramifying and interacting with other collective consumption inequalities). In other words, the operation and effects of an education market benefit certain class groups and fractions to the detriment and disadvantage of others.
>
> (Ball 1994: 117–18)

Proximity to the school has also been identified as a key factor in school decision making for all, but especially working-class, families (Ball 1993; Ball *et al.* 1995, 1996). In theory, open enrolment provides the opportunity for a kind of double selection process. Parents can 'shop' in the school market place and schools can select pupils according to whichever criteria they choose to adopt. Hence open enrolment potentially disassociates the school from an immediate sense of the local or the community. Their 'community' may be widened to encompass pupils and parents from outside a spatial locality.

The notion of choice is now a central tenet of contemporary educational policy and philosophy, in England and Wales (and elsewhere, see Hatcher 1998). Parents have a right to express a preference for the school they wish their child to attend, and this preference is no longer bound by the proximity of the school to home. The diversity of the school market place is not only the result of open enrolment and the local management of schools. Other kinds of state school have also been encouraged, and made real by policy imperatives. For example, grant maintained (GM) schools remained within the auspices of the state, but substantially reduced their links with LEAs. Schools can choose to opt out of LEA control completely, enter into a direct (grant) relationship with central government, enjoy a degree of autonomy, and a reduced relationship with the state. GM schools maintain links with the state, but are able to function in a similar way to private educational systems – exercising more choice over school entrants, and not bound by much of the local government bureaucracy. Schools that cater for different kinds of pupil, such as city technology colleges and specialist schools, have also compounded the diversification of the educational market place. Although these are relatively small in number they contribute to the overall diversity of state schooling, theoretically encouraged as part of the market rhetoric of choice. City technology colleges (Walford and Miller 1991) were set up to provide certain kinds of technological education. The specialist schools programme does not mean schools can opt out of providing the national curriculum, but skews activities towards particular strengths – such as languages, the arts, technology or sport. (It should be noted of course that England and Wales has continued to maintain a small private school sector throughout this period of reform, forming part of an established schools market place in which the politics of choice are readily played out – see Gorard 1997a.)

A result of these changes has been to recast parents (and their children) as educational consumers; individuals that are engaged in choice about educational consumption. This has meant that more information has needed to be made available in the market place, to enable these choices to be made. The success or otherwise of these policies relies (at least in part, and in theory) on parents making rational and informed choices. The ideology of the market place assumes all parents *can* exercise choice, given the necessary information. The publication of more information about schools has largely been government-led, and to a lesser extent provider-led, and designed to inform the rational consumer. Open enrolment, pupil-led funding and parental choice has demanded that schools and the state provide more information in order that schools can be compared. Aside from individual school prospectuses and literature, the state has responded by placing school inspection reports in the public arena, and putting together school league tables, enabling comparisons of schools on the basis of academic performance, and public examination entry and achievement. Of course, while these kinds of publications may be used by parents in making choices, they have also been part of a state drive toward enforcing and demonstrating educational standards, or conversely identifying schools in difficulty or failing (see Chapter 2). League tables and inspection reports identify both the good and the bad, the succeeding and the failing. Ironically, as David (1999: 221) points out, the naming and shaming of poor schools 'also has the effect of demoralising the schools, teachers, parents and children in those schools thus identified' (see Chapter 2).

In considering the range of salient changes to contemporary education in England and Wales it is clear that the educational landscape has been redrawn in recent times. In particular, the shift to an educational market place or quasi-market is significant, and indeed shows no signs of being effectively dismantled under the present administration(s). This new order of education encapsulates and exemplifies broader societal shifts and undertakings. The educational market place serves as an example of 'state craft' (Brown 1997), an increased emphasis on consumption and certification, and an explicit requirement to adopt marketing strategies. These points are elaborated on below:

• *'State craft'*. This is a term used by Brown (1997) to capture the ways in which education has increasingly been utilized by government as a mechanism for electioneering and securing the support of the electorate. Education has increasingly become part of the 'state craft' of government. Woods *et al.* (1998) provide illustrations of this phenomenon, suggesting that a change in government in Britain from Conservative to Labour has not resulted in fundamental changes of policy. Rather the quasi-market in education, with attendant concerns of school diversity, specialization and choice has been reconceptualized as part of the New Labour state craft. The emphasis may have shifted from the rhetorics of individualization and the free market to those of partnership, cooperation, and goodness of fit. But the resultant policies and practices appear remarkably similar to what has gone before. Hence the change in philosophy has not necessarily meant changes in outcome.

- *Consumption.* Education is now firmly established within the realms of consumption; schools are supplied and consumed. State education can be conceptualized in terms of stakeholders, consumers, clients and providers. This carries with it implications for how schools are 'sold', and how consumer voices are assured and heard. Consumption also entails choice and risk. The rhetoric of increased choice has led, in part, to a diversity of educational provision. Fragmentation of the state education system has occurred, at least at the edge. Parents, as consumers, engage in individualized choices (Beck 1992). At the same time schools are involved in semiotic strategies in order to attract and secure consumers (Gewirtz *et al.* 1995). Both providers (schools) and consumers (parents) are engaged in a risky business: schools in making the 'perfect' pitch to encourage consumers to apply, parents in undertaking to choose the 'best school' for their children.
- *Certification.* The changing nature of the education system can be seen in part to be a response to a changing demand for academic qualification. The restructuring of occupations, and economic life more generally, has increased the importance of certification. Notions of parental choice, more 'consumer' information and an ever-increasing concern with standards have privileged the role of the school in the production of 'qualified' individuals. The concern with examination performance and a privileging of the academic can be seen as part of broader shifts. Changes occurring in the social and economic structure of contemporary society have altered the claim for academic qualifications. In turn, a concern with credentialization has forced the state to address the ability of schools to (re)produce a credentialized society. Thus beyond individual parents stating preferences, and individual schools marketing themselves, the shifts in education policy and practice can be articulated in terms of broader concerns about the requirements of education to meet the demands of post-industrial society. Choice making is thus positioned as academically and credentially led (although the reality shows the processes of choice to be much more complex than choosing the school that is perceived to provide the appropriate academic credentials).

In the next section the role of parents in these new educational times is considered, the politics of choice situated within the contexts of social stratification and parent power.

Choice, parentocracy and power

The shift toward educational parentocracy (Brown 1997) was not part of an emergent groundswell from parents, nor was the objective of the school choice reforms explicitly about parent power in the curriculum. Rather the increased 'choice' allocated to parents (as consumers) during the 1980s and

1990s was part of broader education concerns. Brown (1997) suggests that these included concerns over declining standards, and meeting the changing needs of industry and the economy. Schools were perceived to be failing to meet the needs of their pupils, and there was a growing realization that mass investment in education during the twentieth century had not resulted in economic efficiency (nor equal opportunities for that matter, although these were not peddled as a priority of school choice reforms). While commentators have considered the ways in which parents have experienced the shift to a market economy in education, the issue of parental power has remained rather elusive (Fitz *et al.* 1993; David *et al.* 1994; Deem *et al.* 1994; Gorard 1997a, b). Todd and Higgins (1998) argue that the parent–school partnership has remained relatively powerless, serving as a tool of the state rather than as a source of power. Brown (1997) distinguishes between control and responsibility. Parentocracy has increased the onus of responsibility on parents and schools to raise educational standards and achieve satisfactory educational outcomes, while the state has, if anything, excluded parental control over the organization and content of schooling. Thus the educational market place – and in particular the phenomenon of 'choice' – has released the state of the responsibility for pupil rolls and selection, but has not necessarily given parents and schools the opportunities for control over what is taught and how. This is not a new phenomenon, nor restricted to Britain. Ball (1994) suggests that the USA have been stronger on the issue of parental empowerment although, as Fine (1997) has argued, 'parental involvement' projects in the USA have considered different ways of involving parents in education and schooling, but have rarely been about redressing the balance of power. Research on parental choice has revealed the complex ways in which that choice is undertaken, as well as some of the consequences. Research has focused on a variety of parameters around the ideal and the realities of school choice – including the process of choice, the bases of choice and decision making and who actually undertakes the choosing.

Stratification and choice

It is clear that different families approach the decision-making process in different ways (Ball *et al.* 1995; Glatter *et al.* 1997; Gorard 1997a, b). Much of the analysis of school choice has focused on the relationships between social class and choice, and has suggested a class-based dichotomy of those families (parents) who are able to participate in the decision-making process of the educational market place, and those who are not. Edwards *et al.* (1992) have argued that a market ideology sets up a model of ideal parenting, and fails to take into account access to choice. While it would be crude to apply a simple class differentiation here, between middle-class and working-class families, studies have regularly concluded that school choice does involve the appropriation of social/cultural capital and the capacity and opportunity to become informed in order to make real choices – and that these are differentiated along class lines (Ball 1994; Gewirtz *et al.* 1995; Woods *et al.* 1998). Gewirtz and her colleagues have consistently argued that choice is a major factor in maintaining and reinforcing social class inequalities in the school sector.

This body of work has been the subject of some criticism – on two distinctive levels. First, Tooley (1997) has heavily criticized the work of Ball, Gewirtz and Bowe, mainly in terms of their application of qualitative methodology and the conclusions they draw from qualitative data (for a detailed discussion of this critique and debate see Chapter 8). Second, and perhaps more constructively for our purposes here, a number of commentators have highlighted the sheer complexity of decision-making processes that an overemphasis on class differentials may mask. To be fair, however, almost all of the school choice studies have emphasized the complexity of school choice, and the limitations of overgeneralization. Carroll and Walford (1997) have, for example, demonstrated the levels of complexity and diversity of choice strategies, drawing on qualitative interviews with 32 parents whose children are about to move to secondary school. Carroll and Walford contrast 'active' and 'passive' market participants but acknowledge the diversity of responses, and argue that failure to stress complexity is a criticism that could be levelled at other school choice research. Carroll and Walford's analysis does, however, lend support to the reproduction of social inequalities in the educational market place, and decision-making processes:

> Whereas a lack of market resources did not necessarily indicate a 'passive' response to choice, it was clear that a lack of 'cultural capital', or particularly the existence of a different belief system, was more likely to mean inactivity in the educational market place. Many of the families towards the 'passive' end of the continuum lacked full awareness of how the choice process worked in practice.
>
> (Carroll and Walford 1997: 23)

Carroll and Walford (1997) and Thrupp (1999), among others, have suggested that a possible impact of parental choice is an increase in socio-economic stratification between schools, and increased homogeneity in the social composition of schools. This, of course, goes against one of the 'equality' arguments for parental choice – whereby participation in school choice processes may lead to the erosion of social segregation, and a better social mix for schools no longer reliant upon local (homogeneous) enrolment. Through a study of intake data of South Wales secondary schools, Gorard and Fitz (1998) responded to questions of whether school socio-economic stratification is increased in this era of parental choice. They concluded that 'schools in South Wales are generally becoming less stratified over time' (p. 373) and that 'popular schools are . . . increasing their proportion of children from economically disadvantaged families, although this may represent a selection of the most motivated among poor families' (p. 374). Gorard and Fitz are not dismissive of claims that choice and social stratification may be linked in some way. Nor do they suggest that their analysis necessarily lends weight to the case that the market in education is working towards equality of access or opportunities. Rather, Gorard and Fitz argue that analysis of statistical data related to student intake, and variables relating to social class, reveal that simple class–choice equations are inadequate in describing and explaining the complexities of choice, and resultant school mix.

Micro politics of choice

Who actually undertakes school choice, and the basis on which that choice is made, have formed integral questions of various school choice studies. Gorard (1997a, b) developed a model of choice, based on a large-scale study in South Wales. This model articulates the range of relationships between the school choice partners – parents, children and the school. In this model, three components of the choice process are identified, and different roles for the participating partners drawn at each stage. Gorard's (1997b) three-stage model is summarized below.

1 Parents decide on a type of school. This may reflect their own schooling, the schooling of siblings (and affordability/desire to use the fee-paying sector). Aspects such as convenience (for parents), style of education, size of school/ classes, and child welfare are some of the main determinants of choice here.
2 Parents consider alternatives within the type of school identified, and select a subset. They may draw on advice from the current school their child attends, as well as the local reputations of schools, school-based literature, range of facilities and equipment for academic subjects, *and* educational outcomes (for example, known performance indicators such as examination results).
3 Parents *and* children together agree on a specific school. Determinants of choice here may include sports and extra-curricular resources, convenience (for the child), prospects for child's happiness, friendship groups as well as general welfare, and educational outcomes.

Gorard does not represent this model as a linear sequence applicable to all families. Steps can be skipped, and families engage to a lesser or greater extent. Gorard uses the model in order to generate a number of different pathways through which a particular family may go, from those who do not engage in the choice process at all to those 'idealized consumers' who formally consider each step (this has resonance with the model of 'ideal parenting' suggested by Edwards *et al.* 1992). Different families will empower the different generations to a lesser or greater extent. What we are really concerned with here are the micro politics of school choice. While parents and children may both claim to be involved in the choice process, they are usually engaged at different stages and in different ways. Moreover, children and parents tend to highlight *different* reasons for selecting a school. Hence, the distinction between those parents who are engaged and those who are not engaged in the market is overly simplistic of complex choice processes. This also raises questions about the notion of rational choice, on which the ideology of the market is based. While factors such as academic standards and economic outcomes form part of the school decision-making process, other factors (such as locality, friendship groups and local knowledge about the school) also play a part (Ball and Vincent 1998).

The issue of school choice and social class has also been analysed from gendered perspectives (David *et al.* 1994; Reay 1998). In this literature the role of the mother in the educational market place and in the processes of school choice has been emphasized. As David *et al.* (1994) note, mothers are usually involved in school choice processes and procedures, regardless of the kind of child and family. The role of mothers as consumers in the educational market place has been explored. For example, Reay (1998) draws on empirical data of mothers' involvement in the children's primary schooling, and considers the role of mothers in the processes of social (re)production occurring in school contexts. In particular she links class and gender by demonstrating the ways in which especially middle-class mothers are better able to utilize resources in order to practise as effective consumers. She locates this within the more general context of mothers being more involved in the everyday education of their children, and middle-class mothers in particular. 'While the educational system is increasingly shaping the time mothers and children spend together across the social classes, there was only evidence of reciprocal influence among middle class homes and schools' (Reay 1998: 207). Hence gender and class intersect in school choice and parental involvement processes.

Parent power?

Reay's analysis suggests that some parents, in this case middle-class mothers, are better able to influence the education of the children through school involvement. This concords with school choice studies which has indicated that middle-class parents are in a better position to exercise their right to choose, and hence better placed to gain more from the choice reforms (Ball *et al.* 1995; Waslander and Thrupp 1997). Brown's (1990, 1997) analysis of the ideology of parentocracy, and the shift toward this in the UK (and elsewhere) goes further, arguing that the implications for educational selection are substantial. In particular Brown highlights the new bases on which educational opportunity and equality are reconfigured under the mantle of parentocracy:

> Egalitarian principles have already been tried and found wanting. In the educational parentocracy, selection will be determined by the free play of market forces, and because the State is no longer responsible for overseeing selection, inequalities in educational outcome, at least in official accounts, cannot be blamed on the State. Such inequalities (the Right prefer the term 'diversity') will be viewed as the legitimate expression of parental preferences, differences in innate capacities, and a healthy 'diversity' of educational experience.
>
> (Brown 1997: 404)

An implication of the research on parents and school choice is thus that some parents are more able to exercise the right to choose, and in doing so are maintaining and (re)producing stratification at school level. Even bearing in mind the cautions to this understanding (see Gorard and Fitz 1998), the question remains as to how this fits into the overall power relations between families and schools. As Brown (1990) has noted, school choice gives responsibility to parents but not necessarily power. There is a long tradition of home–school liaison and involvement, not least the recent home and school agreements policy in England and Wales (DfEE 1998a; Crozier 1999).

Moreover, the relationships between parents and schools have been the subject of critical scrutiny in recent times (Vincent 1996; Power *et al.* 1998b; Todd and Higgins 1998). In an analysis of case studies of parental involvement in schools, Stanley and Wyness (1999) consider the relationships between teachers and parents in contexts where parental involvement occurs. They argue that parents and teachers pursue their own interests in the context of parental involvement, and that 'the advantage seems to lie with the teachers, and parental empowerment seems to be something of a myth' (Stanley and Wyness 1999: 155). Parental involvement is situated within parent–teacher relationships, whereby the teachers maintain control. This supports research that has highlighted the potential and real powerlessness of parents in educational partnerships (Vincent 1996; Todd and Higgins 1998; Crozier 1999). In critiquing the discourse of partnership between parents and schools/teachers, Heywood-Everett (1999: 167) suggests a partial partnership as 'parents are being invited to be partners in areas outside the critical and empowering areas of school effectiveness, those that have a purchase in the processes of education'. At most, parents do not see themselves as partners at all, and that 'such initiatives as Home and School Agreements have failed to consult fully with parents as to how they preserve their positions *vis-à-vis* a partnership, itself indicative of a lack of partnership in existence' (Heywood-Everett 1999: 168). Parent–teacher consultations, during established parent's evenings for example, have not been widely studied. However they too seem to exacerbate rather than diminish power boundaries:

> In their overall structure, these consultations – which were remarkably similar across schools and individuals – seem to confirm a view of teachers as the participants who hold the power in the interaction. Teachers' acknowledged right to hold the floor at the outset in order to deliver an uninterrupted 'diagnosis', and their recourse to specialist terminologies and paraphernalia (reading ages, tests scores, grade predictions, coursework folders, etc.) established their expert status, as those who have access to relevant knowledge about the student, and therefore the entitlement to exercise professional judgement about their prospects and problems.
>
> (MacLure and Walker 2000: 21)

Commentators such as Todd and Higgins (1998) have documented the differential hierarchies of power that can exist in teacher–parent partnerships, and have recognized that teachers too may experience feelings of powerlessness, to which they may be reacting, under recent government legislation. Power and powerlessness is not a straightforward dichotomy. While the cultural capital of some groups of parents mean they are 'able to rise above their usually powerless position' (Todd and Higgins 1998: 235), partnerships between parents and teachers/schools remain inequitable relations of power – not normally skewed in favour of parents. This is an important consideration in assessing claims of parental involvement and power which have come about as a result of moves toward the quasi market and the increasing consumerization of education – where parents are portrayed as the active and discerning consumers. The notion of school consumption is explored in the next section, which considers some of the ways in which schools have responded to the imposition of a market place.

Marketing the school

The establishment of quasi-markets in education has meant that schools have increasingly had to focus on the maintenance of their pupil numbers. Competition for pupils (and bearing in mind that some pupils and parents are more desirable than others) has required state schools to adopt kinds of marketing strategy, locating themselves within particular market niches which demonstrate something of their values, ethos and (striven for or actual) status. Studies have sought to explore the response of schools to a climate of choice and competition (Gewirtz *et al.* 1995; Woods *et al.* 1998; Maguire *et al.* 1999). The parental and school choice interaction (PASCI) study, for example (Woods *et al.* 1998), undertook research in 11 secondary schools in England. The study concluded that the adaptation of schools had been largely at the level of local organization, rather than major structural shifts. The changing ways in which schools have sought to promote themselves in the educational market place forms part of their response. The schools which were part of the PASCI study put considerable efforts into providing attractive, positive images of themselves, and finding ways of meeting potential pupils and parents. Strategies included open days and open evenings for primary school pupils and parents, and the production of brochures, prospectuses and videos. This is what Gerwirtz *et al.* (1995) have referred to as the glossification of the school; whereby schools have increasingly (re)produced themselves in 'glossy' imagery – using well-established marketing strategies. Aside from open events and the production of publicity materials, schools have also adopted other strategies, such as participation in community events that are designed to promote the school, local press advertising and developing links with preferred feeder schools. This has flowed over into concerns about the physical appearance of the school building (and pupils/students) and the external visibility of the teaching staff (Woods *et al.* 1998). Teachers are increasingly viewed as ambassadors of the school, as well as classroom practitioners. Schools have also become increasingly engaged in what Woods and his colleagues have termed environmental scanning; undertaking to find out and 'assess' the market place of the school – this may include both informal scanning (word of mouth, discussions at open days and school visits) and formal scanning using survey data.

Marketing or selling the school has become a necessary part of the educational landscape, and it has not been without benefit. Schools have had to address their infrastructure, buildings, discipline and pastoral records, as well as measurable academic standards as part of their marketing strategies. The particular focus on academic achievement records has led schools to address academic weaknesses and capitalize on strengths (see Chapter 2). Things that schools always did, such as making links with primary schools, organizing parental visits and so forth (see Delamont and Galton 1986; Measor and Woods 1994) have taken on new importance, and hence such activities have tended to become better organized, with clearer structures and objectives. It could indeed be argued that schools are more in 'touch' with their clients than ever before. Indeed, this would be a view taken by policy makers and proponents of the educational market place. Schools, and their current and future consumers, can benefit from schools learning to address their strengths and weaknesses, and reinforcing their espoused values.

There is, though, another way of approaching the question of schools needing to promote themselves in order to compete effectively and secure their funding in the volatile and fluid educational market place. Waslander and Thrupp (1997), describing this phenomenon in the New Zealand education system, refer to the paradox of marketing. They argue that one consequence of this emphasis on marketing has been to exacerbate the socio-economic segregation between schools. The paradox is that schools with the most educational needs have been forced to give (or waste?) the most time and resources in marketing in order to survive. They have the most to lose if they do not attract students, and yet have had to devote the most to promotional activities. This compounds the argument that the openness and inclusivity suggested by a requirement to market the school is mediated by other constraints of the market place – to increase academic performance and strengthen visible achievements (Woods *et al.* 1998). Marketing may leave personal, social and pastoral aspects of schooling in a potentially vulnerable and ambiguous position. A focus on academic performance and school success, conceived in conventional ways (such as examination and assessment achievement, or 'good' students) may lead schools toward pursuing a strategy of social targeting, rather than true open enrolment (Walford 1994; Thrupp 1999). Studies of established markets in education have noted the equality and social justice issues of this aspect of the educational market place (see Gorard 1997a; Maguire *et al.* 1999). In comparing the fee-paying school market in South Wales with contemporary trends in the UK State sector Gorard (1997a: 254) concluded that

> If state schools . . . spend increasing amounts on promotion, education as a whole may be the loser, whatever the benefits of choice for the individual. An education market is a zero-sum game. As one school wins, another loses, and so as schools put more and more into marketing, they may, like Alice in Wonderland, find themselves running faster and faster just to keep up.

Maguire and her colleagues have undertaken research on the post-16 educational market in the UK. In considering the ways in which post-16 provision is marketed and promoted they argue that market factors do semiotic work as class taste markers. In considering brochures and open days, Maguire *et al.* (1999) analysed the ways in which schools and colleges publicize and promote themselves and their courses. It was clear that 'aspects of niche marketing and targeted promotion were taking place' (1999: 306) and that marketing had a role in the (re)production of social differentiation within the further education sector:

> Clearly, the role of marketing in the reproduction of social differentiation in FE is only one factor among several which contribute to the

'classing' and 'racing' of institutions, but its importance is growing. Increasingly, as education is subject to the processes of commodification, the differences between educational choice and other acts and forms of consumption are being blurred.

(Maguire *et al.* 1999: 306)

The relative balance of formal marketing and promotional strategies in comparison to informal 'grapevine knowledge' (social networks, informal information, rumour, gossip and so forth) has also been addressed:

In the face of what for many parents are the constantly shifting uncertainties of school choice, the grapevine offers some indications, some pointers for the way ahead. Through engagement with the grapevine, parents can feel more firmly embedded in their choice, confirmed in it by the opinions and choices of their friends and relatives.

(Ball and Vincent 1998: 391–2)

It is open to question whether the marketization of schools has led to any overarching cultural transformation. Gorard (1997a: 254) noted in the fee-paying sector that the market had the result of 'pulling toward similarity of provision, with some evidence that larger schools are establishing a quasi monopoly. The fragmentation of the sector, and the lack of a co-operative infrastructure, may presage what will happen in the state sector.' The PASCI study (Woods *et al.* 1998) revealed the degrees to which responses to the market differed from school to school, and between school managements. Like other commentators Woods and colleagues emphasize the complexity and variety of local educational markets and the standpoint and engagement of the schools within these markets (see Walford 1994; Ball *et al.* 1995, 1996; Gewirtz *et al.* 1995; Glatter *et al.* 1997). However, they note that 'one of the effects of the public market as formed in the early 1990s has been to encourage the attention of school managers to move not in the direction of a broader conception of education but towards one that underplays the non-academic experience of schooling' (Woods *et al.* 1998: 207). Gewirtz *et al.* (1995) identified some overarching principles resulting from the glossification of the school. Based on their research on markets and choice in education in Greater London, they argue that one principle has been an (over-)emphasis on academic achievement and performance. This strengthens particular messages about the purposes and objectives of schooling (what counts). They also chart the substantial financial resources and teacher time and energy that are diverted away from educational activities, towards marketing, promoting and the 'ambassadorial' role; and the shift in the nature of the relationship between parents and schools. While the rhetoric is of informing parents, Gewirtz *et al.* argue that what is actually happening is an exercise in attraction by manipulating the image of the school.

Conclusion

The reforms, which have led to the consolidation of the quasi-market place in education, have had a number of consequences, some contradictory in

nature. There is little doubt that the past two decades have seen the diversification of school provision, and this can provide a framework to increase
choice and to ensure a better fit between educational needs and tailored
provision. Moreover, as schools (and other institutions in further and higher
education) have been faced with marketing themselves, issues such as academic standards, infrastructure, and welfare provision have had to be addressed head on. The reforms have also raised concerns about social justice,
equity and power, as well as the role of schooling in contributing to the
teacher and student identities (see Chapter 5). There is evidence to suggest
that choice is not evenly distributed, and that some parents, pupils, students, schools and communities are losing out. It is still difficult to argue
that the auspices of school choice have universal and unequivocal benefits
for all. However, proponents of school markets may well argue that, in the
UK at least, the school market place is partial and therefore less effective
than it might be (Tooley 1995, 2000), and there is little doubt that some
consumers *have* been able to exercise effective choice. Marketing schools is
a mixed process, commanding resources and the development of expertise
to which some schools have better access than others. Rarely is the 'value-
added' potential of schools given prominence over academic performance
(see Chapter 2), and teachers are often faced with adding 'publicity' to their
already burgeoning portfolios. Lastly, it still remains the case that while
parents are increasingly conceptualized as consumers, their status is relatively
powerless, in all but a minority of cases. The reforms around choice and the
educational market place are located within wider changes to public services
and the reformation of relations between the state, social institutions,
professions and private individuals. The next chapter expands this analysis
further, through a consideration of educational knowledge.

4 Educational knowledge(s) *and the* school curriculum

Introduction

The legitimation and reproduction of knowledge play central roles in the overall aims, as well as in the everyday practices of education. As a social process, education is concerned with the transmission of various kinds of knowledge. This knowledge is (re)produced, transmitted and mediated through the relationships between teachers and learners, within institutional contexts and frameworks (of, for example, the school and the curriculum). This chapter explores these contexts and frameworks, and attempts to problematize the concept of educational knowledge. What counts as knowledge is not straightforward. There are a number of ways in which the idea of knowledge can be analysed (and challenged) within contemporary educational contexts. For example, curriculum content is often defined and determined; state guidelines and policy directives can prescribe what actually gets taught in schools. National or core curricula identify a specific knowledge base, and often a preferred mode of transmission. Within and between educational institutions, knowledge can be differentiated and stratified. Not all pupils are afforded the same access to subject knowledge (differentiated by gender or ability, for example). School subjects can also be stratified as high-status or low-status (see Ball 1981; Paechter 1998). Distinctions may also be drawn between official and other forms of knowledge. These questions of definition are compounded by critiques offered by postmodernist and post-structuralist agendas that serve to challenge the very idea of knowledge (Ball 1993; Weiner 1994; Middleton 1995; Apple 1997; Moore and Muller 1999). They do so by implying 'a form of perspectivism which sees knowledge and truth claims as being relative to a culture, form of life, or standpoint and, therefore, ultimately representing a particular perspective and social interest rather than independent, universalistic criteria' (Moore and Muller 1999: 190).

Knowledge is pivotal to our understanding of the relations between education and the state, and the everyday work of the classroom teacher. This is reflected in the various debates and approaches to knowledge within the sociology of education that have been ongoing since the 1970s (and indeed previously). 'Official' legitimated knowledge, as laid down by the state and realized through educational or school contexts, has been subject to a small but sustained critique (and compared alongside other knowledge claims). Moreover teachers, schools and colleges have increasingly been seen as vehicles for the reproduction and transmission of multiple knowledges. This serves as a recognition that official curricula account for only part of what gets taught and learnt in formal educational contexts.

Sociological work on the school curriculum, and knowledge more generally, is usually dated to the early 1970s, and the New Sociology of Education (Young 1971; Moore and Muller 1999) although, as Burgess (1986: 202) has indicated, this view 'overlooks the earlier interventions that were made by sociologists and other commentators'. What Young and his colleagues (see especially Esland 1971; Bernstein 1971) did at the beginning of the 1970s was to place knowledge and the curriculum as central to the processes and project of education. The theorists and educationalists associated with this new sociology of education made explicit the relationships between (educational) knowledge, social control and cultural reproduction. They raised questions about knowledge and the curriculum, and considered the mechanisms by which knowledge is selected, classified and transmitted within the education system, and how this in turn reflects social control and the distribution of power (Bernstein 1971). As Moore and Muller (1999: 190) describe:

> The New Sociology of Education produced a critique of insulated knowledge codes by adopting a 'sociology of knowledge' perspective that claimed to demystify their epistemological pretensions to cognitive superiority by revealing their class base and form. Knowledge relations were transcribed as class relations.

This approach has since given rise to, and been subsumed by, complementary strategies of knowledge analysis. Knowledge relations have also been revealed as gender relations and race relations (Cody *et al.* 1993; Weiner 1994; Fordham 1996; Paechter 1998; Coffey and Delamont 2000). Postmodernist and post-structuralist approaches have consolidated these perspectives, disrupting the claims to universal knowledges based on scientific truths, relating knowledge to issues of power and agency, and utilizing the concepts of discourse and discursive practices in the construction and production of knowledge (cf. Foucault 1974, 1982). This recognizes that individuals are active in engaging in discourses through which they in turn are shaped (Weiner 1994), and that discourse(s), knowledge and power are intertwined:

> In other words we are already subjects and our everyday lives, socially, culturally and institutionally are made up of webs, spirals, waves of discourses which are fluid and shifting, which compete or co-exist and which are always related through these webs. The positioning of an individual with regard to these competing discourses is discursive; that is, individuals can be placed with reference to a number of discourses and be situated in a number of ways.
>
> (Haw 1998: 25)

Hence there are long-standing and contemporary debates over the kinds of knowledge legitimated by/through formal education, and the balance of control over these knowledges. Theoretical perspectives on the sociology of the curriculum have been concerned with exploring the ways in which curriculum content, pedagogical style, and latterly the discursive practices of the curriculum (Bernstein 1990; Haw 1998), contribute to the processes of social, cultural and economic reproduction (Bourdieu and Passerson 1977; Apple 1982). This has involved a consideration of the ways in which knowledge is hierarchically organized, how it is transmitted, to whom and when. Some knowledge domains have been seen as superordinate in relation to others (Bourdieu 1993). Paechter (1998: 64) locates this within what she describes as the 'hegemony of reason and rational thought', arguing that the knowledge that is taught in schools is reasoned or decontextualized knowledge. Paechter maintains that it is decontextualized knowledge that is valued in educational arenas, and that this takes precedence over other kinds of knowledge. Utilizing the concept of 'situated knowledge', Stanley and Wise (1993) locate knowledge within social and cultural contexts. Following Paechter's argument, normal educational arenas do not legitimate knowledge located in everyday practices and contexts. Hence 'contextualized' knowledge, emotional knowledge, 'non-rational' knowledge are negatively framed in formal curriculum discourse. Of course, sociologists and educationalists have long acknowledged the ways in which the everyday practices of school and classroom life contribute to learning, and the ways in which this is distinct from the formal curriculum. This has often been referred to as the hidden or para-curriculum of schooling (Burgess 1986; Measor and Sikes 1992). Feminist commentators, in particular, have acknowledged the situatedness and social positioning of all knowledge claims, and have located knowledge within political processes of certification, superordination and subordination. Weiner (1994: 99), for example, writes of the dominant discourse of knowledge; 'the knowledge that is produced as truth is the knowledge that is linked to the system which produces and sustains it'. Weiner shows how power relationships and subjectivities are reconstituted through discursive practices, arguing that

> the curriculum is central to the production and maintenance of any political and social regime. Curriculum is also heavily implicated in the production of regulative understandings: it is as much concerned about what it means to be an intelligent pupil, a loyal worker or the good mother as about the legitimization of certain forms of knowledge.
>
> (Weiner 1994: 100)

The relationships between teachers and the legitimization of and control over knowledge have been the subject of scrutiny and debate. As Giroux (1988) has argued, the legitimization and reproduction of social knowledge is inscribed in the voices and actions of teachers. This is not necessarily the same as ascertaining that teachers have social control over which knowledge is deemed to be the appropriate realm of the classroom and the school. Teachers' control over 'classroom' knowledge has always been questionable, as teachers are usually working within state-regulating frameworks and with prescribed curricular texts. Teachers' control over knowledge (and indeed how it is transmitted) has increasingly come to be questioned, with the perceived increase in centralization of state education systems and curriculum content/

practices. In England and Wales, for example, the introduction of a national or core curriculum over the past decade or so has been heavily criticized, not least by teacher unions, who have perceived the national curriculum imposition as directly reducing the autonomy and power of teachers over their classrooms (particularly in terms of the curriculum and preferred pedagogic styles). This position has been challenged by, for example, Swann and Brown (1997), who found little evidence that the interpretation of Scotland's national curriculum (the 5–14 development programme) had had an impact on teachers' professional craft knowledge.

Discussions about curricula and knowledge claims are particularly pertinent in the present intellectual climate, and the calls to postmodernism and post-structuralism. The analytical frameworks that these perspectives offer, of local, situated knowledges and claims of no universal 'truths' or 'facts' to be discovered (and transmitted), appear at odds with recent moves to deliver core school curricula, and to increase the rigidity and prescriptiveness of school knowledge. As Apple (1997: 599) has argued,

> With the growth of post-modern and post-structural literature in critical educational and cultural studies . . . we have tended to move quickly away from traditions that continue to be filled with vitality and provide essential insights into the nature of the curriculum and pedagogy that dominate schools at all levels.

In the midst of contemporary knowledge debates, there is perhaps a tendency for postmodernism to 'forget' and lose sight of the role and significance of critical knowledge in the relations between curricula and cultural, social economic capital. Postmodern perspectives can however be useful as a tool in undertaking (sociological) analysis of educational knowledges, and in conceptualizing new approaches to knowledge. This chapter considers the organization, legitimation and transmission of knowledge in educational contexts. It draws on both 'official' and alternative definitions of knowledge, and considers the relationship between knowledge and pedagogy. A discussion of knowledge, and how it is constructed, managed and transmitted is illustrative of the ways in which 'education is going through performed social change in terms of purposes, context and methods' (Usher and Edwards 1994: 3).

The next section explores school knowledge through a consideration of the 'official' curriculum. The chapter then goes on to consider 'other' knowledges embedded within educational arenas, and revisits contemporary knowledge debates.

Curriculum, knowledge and change

It is usual to conceptualize the school curriculum in terms of subject specialism and, indeed, compartmentalization. Common-sense and everyday understandings of school curricula tend to focus around particular subjects, perhaps with some understanding of cross-curricular themes (such as citizenship, for example). Hence a school curriculum and its associated pedagogic practices are conceptualized in terms of discrete packages of knowledge, for example mathematics, history, English literature. However, as Weiner (1994) suggests, 'bodies of knowledge emerge at specific historical moments to account for the "real" or the "natural". Why, we should ask, have mathematics, science, technology and history been so highly prioritized in recent British curriculum formulations?' Across subject specialism or packaging, the curriculum can be conceptualized in broader terms, relating to the knowledge and pedagogical practices that are favoured. Paechter (1998) argues that the school curriculum is inscribed in a particular set of linguistic practices and dominant discourses. Above and beyond individual subjects, school curricula present a package of knowledge, scripted and transmitted in particular ways. Paechter particularly relates this to a consideration of the hegemonic and masculinist nature of 'high-status' school knowledge, but her point can be a more general one, that is, recognizing the power differentials and legitimizing practices inherent in the definitions and transmissions of educational knowledges. The same point is made by Weiner (1994: 98) who describes the curriculum 'as a set of discursive practices in which girls and boys, teachers and pupils, different racial groups are differently and variously constituted as powerful or powerless, good or bad, feminine or masculine, workers or mothers'. To follow this line of argument through, the school curriculum (and its delivery via accepted pedagogic practices) can be conceptualized as one in which dominant discourses seek to normalize some knowledges, and regulate or mute other knowledges.

Here then we have a view of (school) curricula that recognizes the situated, historical, local and discursive contexts of educational knowledges. This can be developed in a number of ways. Paechter (1998: 81) for example considers the relative status of school subjects in English and Welsh schools to argue that 'there has been a long standing tendency for researchers to focus on high status curriculum areas, ignoring those associated with less powerful forms of knowledge'. She argues that some subjects are marginalized – by the comparative status of different kinds of knowledge (a point returned to later in this chapter). Fordham (1996) makes a similar point, by exploring the omissions and deletions of the formal school curriculum in the USA. For example, she points to the implicit and pervasive exclusion from the curriculum of 'everything that might be linked to the Black community' (p. 202), and contrasts the explicit teaching about democracy and equality with the perception that 'virtually every feature of the school curriculum, including textbooks' celebrates otherness (p. 333). Hence Fordham considers how the (re)presentations embodied in school knowledge claims are implicated in the development and resistance of identities (for example, black identities or gendered identities).

A further way of considering the conceptualization of 'school knowledge' is through presentation and transmission strategies. It is relatively unusual for pupils or students to be presented with the problematics of knowledge, or asked how ideas come to be seen as dominant or normal. Rather, it is still the case that school students are presented with knowledges that are relatively desituated and decontextualized. Knowledges transmitted in formal educative settings are set up as truths and universals (Walkerdine 1988, 1989; Paechter 1998). The discourses of learning transmit, rather than seek to challenge, accepted and dominant understandings of the social world and of academic subject disciplines. Particular ideas and sets of knowledges are imparted without critical attention to how they got there or why they are being privileged over other ideas or sets of knowledges (Weiner 1994; Fordham 1996). These arguments are not necessarily about the particular or discrete content of school curriculum subjects; rather, they focus attention on curricular discourses and practices that shape the teaching and learning of school subjects. This provides a framework for considering the discursive *and* linguistic practices of curriculum delivery, as well as the power conceptualizations and relations that are embodied therein. In addition it provides a mechanism for addressing school curricula in terms of social justice and identity issues. Feminist scholars, for example, have pointed to ways in which the assumed knowledge base, and modes of delivery, of school curricula embody gendered understandings and power relations (Walkerdine 1989; Weiner 1994; Commeyras and Alvermann 1996; Paechter 1998). Similar points have been made with regard to the curriculum and issues of race and ethnicity (see for example Cody *et al.* 1993; Fordham 1996; Dei *et al.* 1997; Haw 1998). Such work augments earlier sociological work on the school curriculum which revealed the relationships between linguistic practice, school knowledge and social class (Bernstein 1975, 1990; Bourdieu and Passerson 1977; see also Apple 1997).

School knowledge has been increasingly centralized in the restructuring of education in western societies (Brown *et al.* 1997). In the United Kingdom this centralization has been embodied in the formulation and implementation of national curricula (of which there are similar examples in North America and New Zealand, see Hargreaves 1994; Wylie 1994). National curricula in England and Wales were introduced, following the 1988 Education Reform Act (broadly the same, but with the Welsh language incorporated in the Welsh schemes). Scotland has had a nationally recommended curriculum framework from 1977, and a common core curriculum (5–14), actioned through negotiation between policy makers and practitioners, since the late 1980s. (Northern Ireland has also had a national curriculum since 1989.)

> Despite differences in detail and terminology, the four national curricula appear to be providing a broadly similar curriculum to pupils in each part of the UK. Each national curriculum covers the same subjects or subject areas. The content of subject courses is likely to be broadly similar since the content of academic subjects is determined by subject specialists in the teaching professions and university departments who form a UK-wide, and indeed international, constituency.
>
> (Croxford 2000: 121)

Since the introduction of these UK national curricula, various changes have been made. For example, the English and Welsh national curricula were modified in 1994 and the compulsory elements reduced. This followed considerable protest, not least from the teaching unions. While the Labour administration has not suggested large-scale change, they have highlighted the importance of the national curriculum in shaping entitlement and opportunity, and have also given a heightened priority to basic skills, for example of literacy and numeracy (DfEE 1997; see also Dearing 1994). National curricula provide a mechanism for government to exert direct control over what is taught in schools and how. This is demonstrative of the normalizing and regulating aspects of dominant curriculum discourses. It also epitomizes the symbolic and 'real' link between school knowledge and the needs of the state. The new curriculum structures, indicated in the national curricula in the UK, have been built on the back of New Right criticisms of both educational philosophy and practice, 'influenced more by the conservative political agenda than educational or egalitarian principles' (Croxford 2000: 115). One interpretation of this is that schooling has been increasingly, rather than decreasingly, recognized as an important site of cultural transmission, with the state playing an increasingly central part in regulating and legitimizing 'appropriate' knowledge transmission. The national curriculum has confirmed the status of school knowledge as something that can be defined, delivered and assessed under discrete headings. A centralized and increasingly prescribed curriculum arguably denies the roles of teachers, students, parents and communities as creators of knowledge, and places the state in the role of arbiter over what counts as the knowledge of/for education, and how it should be assessed and tested. School knowledge, in this context, is divided into key stages and delivered in terms of distinct subject areas (as per the national curriculum). In England and Wales, for example, there are a number of subjects defined as core or compulsory. Non-core or optional subjects augment these. Each key stage and each subject is specified in terms of content and attainment targets, manifested in national curriculum test results (Torrance 1997).

Social justice and equality issues have formed part of the commentary on national curriculum frameworks and implementation. For example, there have been some claims of equal opportunities promotion through national curriculum practice, although these impacts have been viewed as accidental rather than intentional. For example, Croxford (2000: 123) comments on the national curricula in place across the UK:

> A common feature of each national curriculum is that between the age of 5–14 all pupils, regardless of gender, must study required subjects or curricular areas. All pupils are entitled to develop the same learning skills, and experience the same areas of knowledge. This is an important means of ensuring that girls and boys have equal opportunities to learn. In theory, it removes the possibility that schools might make different provision for girls and boys.

The national curriculum effectively removes some of the most differential curriculum choices; the national curriculum logic is that all students regardless of class, gender, race or ability study core subjects. An argument can be made that this has removed the status hierarchies of many school subjects, and related subject 'choices' based on class (gender, race, or ability). Indeed, research for the Equal Opportunities Commission in England and Wales provided concrete evidence of this with regard to gender (Arnot *et al.* 1996; Salisbury 1996; see also Arnot *et al.* 1998). The introduction of the national curriculum, and effective curtailment of substantial curriculum choice up to 16 years, serves (unsurprisingly) to even out gender differences in subject take-up (in England and Wales more choice has subsequently been reintroduced at 14 plus, and this has in turn led to speculation that old differential subject choice patterns will re-emerge – see Paechter 1998).

Any reading of this equal opportunities case for national curricula should be approached with some caution. Croxford (2000: 123) notes that in practice 'the reality of classroom experiences of different areas of the curriculum may still differ for girls and boys, because of the attitudes and behaviours of children and teachers, and the influences of society'. Moreover, studies have consistently shown that, when faced with subject choices, gendered patterns persist, even if these are diluted or less pronounced. Arnot *et al.* (1998), in an Ofsted review of research on gender and educational performance, noted that although there had been a narrowing of the gender gap in patterns of entry to the General Certificate of Secondary Education (GCSE, 16 years), there was not a comparable pattern emerging in post-16 education:

> Indeed, post-16 gender-related patterns have persisted and in some cases increased. In searching for explanations, we need to recognize that the introduction of the National Curriculum has had the effect of *restricting* choice at GCSE, thus encouraging pupils to enter for subjects that they might avoid if they had the choice. After GCSE, these restrictions do not operate and other factors are brought to bear on choices.
>
> (Arnot *et al.* 1998: 31, their emphasis)

Specifically, changes in curriculum choice patterns have been mainly one-directional. There is evidence that 'girls are more prepared to tackle "masculine" subjects, especially high-status subjects; boys, on the other hand, continue to shun "feminine" subjects' (Arnot *et al.* 1998: 31; see also Arnot *et al.* 1996).

Any consideration of the national curriculum must be situated in a political, national and *institutional* context. Formulations of school knowledge as manifested through the national curriculum provide particularly powerful examples of the linkages between the state and the education system (see Avis 1995 for a commentary on changes to the post-compulsory curriculum, and issues of social difference). What/whose knowledge is taught (and how) and the values that are fostered are key considerations. A number of commentators have linked the national curriculum to wider state concerns with the reaffirmation of national identity in the global society (Coulby and Bash 1991). Ball (1994), for example, conceptualizes the national curriculum in England and Wales in terms of struggles between modernizing conservatives, keen to link the curriculum to the changing needs of the economy, and the restorationist conservatives attempting to reassert a national identity. Ball (1994) tips the balance in favour of the restorationists. There is little doubt that the introduction of the national curriculum in England and Wales has brought to prominence certain subjects and ways of conceptualizing those subjects, and has re-established and consolidated the relationship between education, state and national identity. Coulby (1991) identified a number of areas/subjects of the then emergent national curricula in England and Wales that could be perceived as nationalist and/or racist. These included issues around language provision, the provision of history teaching and religious education:

> In some ways the tendency toward nationalism is implicit in the subject-based structure of the National Curriculum, especially given the traditionalist subjects that have been selected for prominence. More integrated thematic approaches such as Global Relations of Health Studies, with an explicit commitment to internationalist, multicultural and anti-racist approaches, were discarded in favour of the traditional grammar school approach.
>
> (Coulby 1991: 31)

History in the school curriculum provides a particularly good example for the exegesis of these debates. The 1990s saw substantial efforts to introduce a national history curriculum to England and Wales, as part of the more general deliberations of formulating a national core curriculum. Coulby (1991: 33) notes that history was the national curriculum subject 'most vulnerable to political interpretation and partisan bias'. The way in which a school system presents the history of the nation state will carry messages about sensitive subjects such as religion, class structures, and patterns of inequality and foreign relations. The development of a national curriculum for history is enmeshed in debates over the relationships between history and particular understandings of nationhood and identity. The development of the national history curriculum in England and Wales also came on the back of New Right backlashes of so-called radical history, accused of denigrating the history of the nation (Thomas 1979), and criticisms of political correctness. In North America a similar process had been underway, and similar debates ensued – emphasizing national triumph and lamenting the de-emphasis of studying chronology and great men (see Weiner 1994; Commeyras and Alvermann 1996). Several commentators have criticized the history provision that was formulated as part of the English and Welsh national curriculum development. Fisher (1990), for example, argued that the provision of world history was limited and biased, and could serve to perpetuate distorted and racist perspectives, a view shared by Coulby (1991). In this restorationist history, Britain was (re)centred as 'a benign and progressive influence upon the world, bearer of justice and civilization' (Ball 1994: 39).

Weiner (1993) provided a social justice analysis of school history, as envisaged in the English national curriculum. She considered the development of the national curriculum during the early 1990s, and analysed the documentation. Her analysis included a review of equality issues and specifically gender, set within the context of the nationalist 'past glories' approach (Ball 1994: 39). The final report of the English national curriculum history working group (DES 1990), tasked with developing the 'new' history curriculum, did pay some attention to equality concerns, though this was rather limited. Only four paragraphs were given over to gender, for example. These were delivered under the guise of equal opportunities (though as Weiner

points out, multiculturalism and race came off worse, with only two paragraphs and an implicit assumption that the more ethnically diverse the
population the more case there is for *British* history within the curriculum).
The working party provided advice on 'the evils of stereotyping and the bias
of "heroic" history' (Weiner 1993: 91), but the prescribed *content* of the
history units to be taught in schools was gender-biased, and did little to
present re-visioned historical accounts of women. Weiner locates these gender issues alongside more general trends in the establishment of a 'national'
curriculum history: the lack of radical or feminist historical perspectives; an
emphasis on content and fact, rather than analytical and historical skills; the
favouring of political and military history at the expense of social and cultural history, and the centring of a 'positive' version of British history. In
conclusion, Weiner ascertained that the 'new' history curriculum presented a
decontextualized 'malestream' white history. This can be seen too in broader
terms, as part of the 'deconstruction of the comprehensive, modernist curriculum and its replacement with a political but depoliticized, authoritative
curriculum of tradition' (Ball 1994: 39). History is highlighted here as a particularly transparent example of the ways in which 'knowledge' is (re)situated
and (re)defined as part of political–education agendas. Theoretical knowledge
taught through the school curriculum should be viewed as representing
particular (but not exclusive) versions of the possible knowledge bias. Moves
toward a national curriculum (albeit the now scaled down/streamlined one)
serve to illustrate the political, national, ideological and social aspects of
situated knowledges, at the same time providing a powerful example of the
relationships between the state and the practices of education. These aspects
become more complicated when the 'para-curriculum' (Burgess 1986) or
informal knowledges of schooling are considered.

Other knowledge(s)

The knowledge enshrined in the 'official' school curriculum is one part of a
much broader knowledge base that teachers (and learners) bring to education. Hence schools (and other educational institutions/settings) are sites for
the transmission and (re)production of other knowledges. We can different-
iate between these knowledges in a number of ways. As has already been
noted, within the formalized 'academic' (or legitimized) curriculum there are
dominant and subordinate discourses at work. School subjects are crafted
and shaped according to these discourses and then positioned within educational structures and institutions. Hegemonic masculinity and racialized
discourses of schooling can be set alongside other aspects of knowledge
stratification (for example, see Coffey and Delamont 2000 for a discussion
of relationships between feminisms and educational knowledge). Distinctions can be made, for example, between academic and less academic subjects; and between the formalized and 'other' (hidden/para) curricula of
schooling. Commentators have distinguished between academic and non-
(or less) academic school subjects, or between dominant and marginal subjects
(Attar 1990; Sparkes *et al.* 1990; Paechter 1998). Paechter's (1998) analysis

concentrates on the 'otherness' of marginal subjects in the curriculum. She chooses to focus on two areas of the school curriculum which she defines as marginal (and which have traditionally been located as non-academic subjects) – craft, design and technology (CDT) (incorporating 'craft' skills and home economics) and physical education (PE). She addresses what it means for the subject (and those who study it) to be marginally located within the school curriculum. She locates the low status of these subjects within their specific gendered and social class histories (working-class girls learning how to cook, working-class boys learning to do manual labour; the differential emphasis of boys' and girls' physical education over time and so on). She points to the ways in which subjects like CDT and PE have also been linked to the less able, the disaffected (and in some cases particular ethnic groups – see Carrington and Wood 1983). Hence 'subject marginality is bound up not only with the comparative status of different kinds of knowledge, but also with images of masculinity and femininity that involve ideas about the body, social class, and the relationship between power, knowledge and the self' (Paechter 1998: 91).

Subject specialist teachers in marginal subjects have been shown to have relatively weak voices within both the school and the educational arena more generally. Paechter's analysis suggests that in these non-academic areas of the curriculum some groups, especially girls, black boys and less able students, are constructed as *Other*. Moreover, subject content reflects this marginal *Other* status. For example, gendered versions of design and technology, and physical education are normalized within the school curriculum:

> The cases of [design and technology, and physical education] make it clear that it is quite possible for alternative male and female forms of a subject to develop and flourish more or less independently for decades, even in mixed schools. The subjects where this has happened however, are those that are themselves *Other* within the school curriculum; they are of low status, and generally aimed at those, often working class, students who are seen as 'less-able'. Higher status subjects only come in one main form; there are no gendered alternatives.
>
> (Paechter 1998: 90)

A particularly good example of this can be drawn from Chessum's (1989) teacher account of Countesthorpe College, a 'democratic' comprehensive school set up in the English county of Leicestershire during the 1970s. In Chessum's ad hoc (extra-curricular) afternoon cookery lessons less able students were able to work outside the context of the specialist, formalized curriculum:

> The group was mostly boys, often but not exclusively less academically involved students who were not able to develop the organisation required to get ingredients together in preparation for the timetabled cookery lessons offered as a specialist subject . . . Students who were habitual 'failures' in academic work often gained self confidence and pride in their cooking . . . they worked alongside a group of three very

academic girls who came occasionally for light relief from their time-table rather crowded with academic subjects.

(Chessum 1989: 125)

Aside from discrete subject knowledges (both academic and less academic), educational arenas also transmit and reproduce mundane or everyday knowledges through their routines, regularities and day-to-day work. These aspects of schooling, outside the formal curriculum, have been termed the hidden or para curriculum (Jackson 1968; Hargreaves 1978; Burgess 1986; Measor and Sikes 1992). Teachers, pupils and students have beliefs and under-standing about how society functions, and these permeate the social fabric of the school. These 'alternative' knowledges appear in different contexts; for example meal times, physical education classes, public 'homilies', and everyday mundane interactions. Aspects of the hidden or para curriculum have been linked to the gendered and racialized discourses of schooling. Hampton (1992), for example, considered the role of school meals in multicultural schools in the UK, and the ways in which food organization and delivery contributed to an increase in cultural distance, and the stereo-typing of British school children as hosts or strangers. Measor (1984) de-monstrated how female pupils' 'folk' beliefs about femininity impeded their science teacher's attempt to get them to do experiments and Delamont (1998) analysed the folk models of gender offered by PE teachers to 12-year-old girls. Riseborough's (1988) account of a cookery teacher in an orthodox Jewish school, where the staff and pupils shared a set of knowledge about the world which was more powerful than the official curriculum, is another classic example. The state has not neglected these tacit areas of educational knowledge transmission. There are a number of areas in which personal, social and moral education has been and continues to be seen as part of the realm of the school (and indeed the curriculum). Three examples are given here, by way of illustration.

The enhanced role of pastoral care within the discourse of the curriculum

Power (1991) has drawn attention to the ways in which pastoral care has become a distinct category of secondary school curriculum provision. While schools have always had an interest in more than the academic education of pupils, Power argues that the categorization of pastoral care as a distinct curriculum area is a relatively recent phenomenon, and linked to wider processes of education and curriculum change. She grounds her analysis in the historical moves away from a nineteenth-century concern with moral and religious education through to an increasing secularization of the curriculum during the twentieth century. Power (1991: 201) argues that the 'successive distancing of the "academic" from issues of moral or social regulation . . . has witnessed their inclusion within the distinct and increas-ingly coherent category of pastoral care'. She argues that pastoral care has been increasingly significant in curriculum discourse in the reorganization of secondary schooling that has taken place over the course of the twentieth century (and in particular as part of the moves to comprehensive schooling in the 1970s):

> The discourse of pastoral care, with its emphasis on individuality, provided a vehicle for an organizing principle based on unique differentiation. Rather than standing in opposition to the scholarly tradition, pastoral care enabled 'academic' stratification to continue and survive within the comprehensive school as only one aspect of many that make up the 'whole child'.
>
> (Power 1991: 206)

This tension between the academic and the pastoral continues to be central to contemporary debates over educational standards on the one hand, and the social, personal and moral development of young people on the other.

Sexual relationship education

Recent debates about the appropriateness of sexual relationship education have brought to the core the links between the state and the personal development of young people. The present UK Labour administration's campaign to remove Section 28 of the Local Government Act (1988) (which actually bans the promotion of homosexuality by local authorities rather than barring the teaching about homosexualities in schools), and the consultation exercise on sex and relationship guidance which the Department for Education and Employment (DfEE) is presently undertaking, serve as contemporary examples of the ways in which the political discourses of sexuality are manifested at the educational and school level. Epstein and Johnson (1998: 45) note the 'successes of moral traditionalist and New Right campaigning on sexual and educational issues' between 1984 and 1996, which served to constrain and disorganize school sex education, and the more recent social liberal discourses which have centred attention on the role of education in teaching and learning about sexual relationships: 'Accordingly, the preferred form of state action is educational. Education for marriage, for parenting or for relationships, elaborated health education programmes, and a liberal sex education in schools and outside have been characteristic social liberal demands' (Epstein and Johnson 1998: 69). The relations between the state, the school and sex(uality) education are complex (see Jones and Mahony 1989; Epstein and Johnson 1998) and currently in revision. They serve to remind us that even the most personal can become part of the school curriculum discourse.

The re-establishment of citizenship education in (and out of) schools

The British government's advisory group on citizenship has recently recommended that citizenship education should be a statutory part of all pupils' education (Citizenship Advisory Group 1998). Hence citizenship has re-emerged as part of the school curriculum agenda although, as Gillborn (1992) has pointed out, schools have always taught a great deal about the realities of citizenship through the hidden curriculum. Citizenship education was formulated as a cross-curricular theme under the England and Wales National Curriculum guidelines of the late 1980s and 1990s (NCC 1990). Education has always provided an important site of transmission for citizenship skills and identities, and this has increasingly been recognized (and legislated for) by recent administrations. However, citizenship has a number of different meanings and interpretations. The definitions of citizenship that have become part of official curricular discourses are at best contentious interpretations of the broader issue. As Connell (1992: 133) has argued,

> The idea of 'citizenship' everywhere has two faces, and nowhere are they more sharply contrasted than in education. On the one hand citizenship appears as a principle of regulation and social order, casting citizens into standardised relations of obedience and orderliness . . . on the other hand citizenship appears as a claim of rights, as a demand by the excluded for access and participation.

Certainly the rhetoric of contemporary education for citizenship encompasses notions of belonging, social inclusion and participation, caught up in a package of active citizenship. How much that rhetoric, translated into official curricula, will map onto the realities of citizenship 'learnt' by students through the everyday processes and practices of schooling is, however, far from clear (see Chapter 6 for a more detailed discussion of citizenship education). Nevertheless, citizenship education, in its various guises, provides a particularly salient example of the ways in which everyday knowledges (and indeed skills) are embedded in, and regulated through, (school) curricula.

Conclusion

This chapter has primarily focused on educational knowledge(s) in the context of school curricula (both formal and 'hidden' or mundane). The school curriculum should be viewed as a fluid and changing scene, rather than necessarily a static entity. It is clear that what 'counts' as the appropriate remit of schools in terms of knowledge transmission (broadly defined) is open to debate and redefinition, to suit social and political agendas, as well as in relation to theoretical positions over the state and status of knowledge claims. Little has been said thus far about the transformative potential of knowledge, yet commentators have highlighted the ways in which bodies of knowledge can disrupt conventional discourses, and even bring about social change. For example Dei (1999) argues that anti-racist knowledge can challenge popular discursive practices, provide for a critical interrogation of conventional, common-sense knowledge and disrupt so-called stable knowledge: 'As an oppositional knowledge, anti-racism has the task of disrupting hegemonic texts and curricular and instructional practices of official school pedagogy, as well as their roles and functions in stabilizing knowledge' (Dei 1999: 406). Feminist scholars and educationalists have also considered the transformative potential of (new) knowledge, and proposed a recasting of curriculum content and pedagogy (see Coffey and Delamont 2000). Hence in considering the role of education in the transmission and (re)production of knowledges we should not lose sight of alternative definers and knowers.

In conclusion I return to the postmodern musings over knowledge claims. In the light of postmodern and post-structuralist critiques which challenge the absolute idea of knowledge, it is easy to dismiss what Apple (1997: 598) terms 'the political economy of what knowledge is considered high status'. While contemporary theoretical and epistemological debates ensue over what counts as appropriate knowledge 'what are commonsensically known as the sciences and technology . . . are receiving even more emphasis in terms of time in the curriculum, funding, prestige, support from apparatuses of the state' (Apple 1997: 598). Hence while the dereification of knowledge has been central to the social sciences, it is important not to lose sight of the realities of knowledge reproduction in the accumulation of cultural and indeed economic/political capital.

Moore and Muller (1999) advance a further critique of the postmodernist discursive concern with 'voice'. In translating knowledge forms and knowledge relations into social standpoints and power relations, Moore and Muller argue that postmodern perspectives are in danger of actually reifying positivistic and 'truth' versions of knowledge:

> It is ironic that the postmodernists, and those now sheltering under their wings, are the only ones left with any interest in positivism. Their account holds only for as long as positivism stands. In this sense, positivism is their secret 'Other' – the orthodoxy that is the condition for their heterodoxy. It is, then, not surprising that they do so much to sustain it in their various accounts of the 'dominant discourse'.
>
> (Moore and Muller 1999: 198–9)

Hence Moore and Muller suggest that postmodern approaches to knowledge (and foreshadowed in earlier sociology of education work on knowledge) are in danger of reproducing a simplistic version of science. In this context, preoccupations with positions, standpoints and voices may serve to 'politically bankrupt' rather than recentre the sociology of knowledge. The discourse of voice, and the centring of experience, is examined further in the next chapter. Chapter 5 explores the narrative turn in sociology (of education), and considers the relationships between education, biography and identity.

5 Identities *and* biographies

Introduction

The relationship between society and the self has become an increasing focus of contemporary sociology. In particular has come a renewed interest in the social processes by which selves are produced and reproduced, crafted and challenged. As Billington *et al.* (1998) note, sociologists are increasingly concerned with the ways in which self-identity is constructed through (and in turn constructs) the processes of social life. Paralleling this sociological concern with the self have been proclamations among academics and intellectuals heralding the arrival (and perhaps passing?) of the postmodern era, and a current vogue for claiming postmodernism as the intellectual movement (and indeed societal shift) of the 1990s. The postmodern challenge to a consensus held among the educated classes in western capitalist nations (since the Enlightenment at the end of the eighteenth century), that universal scientific 'truths' can be reached by scientific methods, is not one with which all commentators would agree (see Coffey and Delamont 2000). However, the postmodern argument that there are no universal truths to be discovered, and that all accounts are necessarily partial, local, historically and culturally grounded, has affected the ways in which we conceptualize relationships between society and the self. Calls for views of the self that recognize the inherent negotiated and interactional qualities have become increasingly acknowledged. No longer (if indeed it ever was) seen as a fixed, static entity, the self is increasingly viewed as dynamic, fluid, 'multiple' and subject to contestation. It has become analytically useful to consider selves that are negotiated, constructed and articulated, and in turn to view individuals as actively part of this process – creating selves that are free-floating and multiple, subject to constant flux and change (Goodson 1997). If we go along with this view of societal shift and the attendant consequences for the self (or selves), then it follows that the processes by which the self is (re)constructed should interest sociologists. Concerned with documenting social life and social change, sociologists (alongside social scientists more generally) have increasingly explored these processes. This has involved conceptualizing the construction and negotiation of selves as the active *work* of social actors, whereby they are engaged in a continuous and dynamic process of identity or biographical work in their everyday social and cultural lives.

This chapter draws on these understandings of identity in contemporary society to explore the everyday work of social actors in educational settings. Educational arenas form important sites for the active engagement of identity and biographical work (Fordham 1996). Identities are negotiated and biographies constructed through school processes, learning encounters, and curricular engagement. In turn, the articulation and representation of selves in educational settings can be challenged, changed, resisted or accepted. The relationship between selves and the structures and processes of education are complex and multifaceted. In the course of this chapter some of these representations of, and challenges to, identity work in educational contexts are considered. The chapter is structured in five sections, each concentrating on a different aspect of identity work and the (re)construction and representation of (educational) biographies. First, a brief overview of the sociological interest in biographical work is given, as a means of contextualizing the chapter and placing it into a broader context of sociological and social change. A second section discusses the now substantial body of work on the relationships between the work of the teacher and the (re)construction of teacher selves. The final three sections of the chapter each explore a specific articulation of educational identity work. Contemporary sociological explorations of gender, sexuality and race in educational contexts are drawn upon in order to consider the ways in which social actors are constantly involved in the processes of identity formation and biographical reproduction.

Sociology and the biographical turn

The social sciences in general, and sociology in particular, have increasingly focused on the ways in which self-identity is constructed and negotiated through complex social processes. This has led to what has been called the 'biographical turn' within sociological inquiry and writing. A critical exploration of the links between science and biography (or identity), and a concern with the ways in which personal narratives and experiences can lead to fruitful sociological data on social processes, are indicative of this approach. There has then been an increasing assumption (especially within, but not confined to, qualitative work) that the personal narrative is able to offer data which are grounded in both biographical experience and social contexts (Atkinson and Silverman 1997). Stanley and Morgan (1993) have highlighted the potential significance of biography in sociological inquiry (see also Plummer 1983, 1995; Denzin 1989, 1997; Erben 1993; Ellis and Bochner 1996). By reconceptualizing identity and biography as work, as topics of investigation (rather than unproblematic resources), and as analytical tools (Coffey 1999), we can challenge

> conventional sharp distinctions between structure and action, and, relatedly, individual and collective, as presenting an over-dichotomised view of social life. It means rejecting any notion that 'a life' can be

understood as a representation of a single life in isolation from net-works of interwoven biographies. In spite of the widespread assumption that autobiography is concerned with a single life, in practice it is a very rare autobiography that is not replete with the potted biographies of significant others in the subject's life.

(Stanley and Morgan 1993: 2)

Stanley (1992) refers to this sociological movement as the biographizing of social structure, and the structuralizing of biography. She argues that, as well as documenting individual lives and identities, the biographical turn in sociological inquiry provides a strategy for exploring personal histories and biographies, as well as the relationships between structure and agency in contemporary society. It should be noted here that a sociological concern with identity and biographical work has not been confined to data that sociologists collect about others. Autobiographical work, writing and reflection have also become part of the sociological endeavour (see Cotterill and Letherby 1993; Ellis 1995; Ronai 1996; Tillman-Healy 1996; Ellis and Bochner 2000). Early collections by sociologists, reflecting on their work and their place within their research and writing, have now been joined by much more personalized accounts. These place the sociologist (and his/her (auto)biography) into the actual work and scope of sociological inquiry (Coffey 1999). This 'revealing of the sociologist' has shifted – from early attempts to make visible the linked personal experiences of sociology (through collections such as Hammond 1964; Bell and Encel 1978; Roberts 1981; McKeganey and Cunningham-Burley 1987) to a centralizing of the autobiographical as a basis for sociological analysis and understanding (see for example collections by Okely and Callaway 1992; Ellis and Bochner 1996; Wolf 1996). The so-called early 'confessional' accounts (Van Maanen 1988) of the naïve incompetent sociologist, or fallible researcher, overcoming adversity, difficulty or illness in the pursuit of data has been replaced by a much more sophisticated understanding of the relationships between social research, sociological writing and the self. Hence in our writing we are also engaged in applying 'critical reflection to our ongoing task of making sense of who we are and what it is we do' (Agar 1986: xi).

The biographical (and indeed autobiographical) turn is not without its critics and cautionary tales. Some commentators have pointed out that utilizing personal narratives and biographies is potentially problematic (Goodson 1992; Atkinson and Silverman 1997; Munro 1998). There is an inherent danger of romanticizing the individual and their stories in biographizing the social, and a possibility of 'missing' the social contexts and processes by overly concentrating on the individual and the personal. By privileging certain voices and lives we may also be charged with ignoring the voices and lives of others (Paechter 1998). In addition, there is a danger of a narcissistic preoccupation with one's own voice and life, to the detriment of those we seek to understand. This is an argument engaged with by Mykhalovskiy (1997), who contends that autobiographical sociology *per se* is not necessarily narcissistic or self-indulgent. He suggests instead that autobiography can be productive to the ways we think about the processes of research, and in the reading and writing of sociological texts. The personal presence in the text can be a source of insightful analysis, reacting against the insularity of academic writing. Nevertheless commentators such as Munro (1998) suggest that, in embracing the biographical turn, we should remain suspicious of claims of privilege, while welcoming the new insights the approach is able to offer. Biographical, sociological work can aid the steering of a course which Stanley (1993: 2) refers to as 'between the over determinism of some varieties of socialization theory, and the opposite extremes of seeing selves as externally unique individuals which are the product of inner psychological processes'. If we assume that a core component of sociology is to understand individuals in social and cultural context, then the biographical turn is a useful aid to this process, albeit one which should be approached with a healthy caution. In the next section this sociological concern with the (auto)biographical is placed in educational context.

Identity work in educational settings

The understanding, (re)creating and representing of lives through the collection and analysis of narratives is now a key component of sociologically informed work within the field of education. Researchers have increasingly paid attention to the biographical work that occurs in educational settings. Schools, and other educational arenas, have increasingly been seen as sites for the active construction, production and reproduction of biographies and identities. Hence life histories, biographical data and personal narratives have been collected and analysed as mechanisms for understanding the lived realities of schools and of teaching (Connelly and Clandinin 1995; Rust 1999). The distinction has been made between the 'telling' of individual lives (of/by individual teachers for example) and making sense of those lives in terms of collective experiences and social processes. Huberman *et al.* (1997: 14), for example, choose to distinguish between biographies and life histories of individual teachers and perspectives which aim 'to create accounts not of individual careers or professional lives, but of patterns in the career paths taken by the teachers studied and of the dynamics that explain these patterns'. Such a distinction for teachers (but equally applicable to students, pupils and their educational careers) is useful in articulating the situated and structural contexts of individual experiences. The collection of personal biographies and narratives gives voice to teachers and their teaching. As Goodson (1981, 1997) has argued, the collectivity of narratives and biographies can lead into a consideration of broader pictures of teaching careers and the teaching profession:

> Studies of the teacher's life and work develop structural insights which locate the teacher's life within the deeply structured and embedded environments of schooling . . . it is true that personal data can be irrelevant, eccentric and essentially redundant. But the point that needs to be grasped is that these features are not the inevitable collection of that which is personal. Moreover that which is personal at the point of collection may not remain personal. After all a good deal of social

science is concerned with the collection of a range of other personal insights and events and the elucidation of more collective and generalizable proffering and processes.

(Goodson 1997: 145)

The social world of education has increasingly been seen, and 'told', in terms of personal narratives and individual experiences. These have been conceptualized in terms of identity and biographical work – and utilized to explore the social and cultural processes of schooling. Social actors within educational arenas (teachers, administrators, managers, students, pupils) have hence been the subjects of this kind of inquiry. Studies have been concerned with exploring the lived realities of education through personal biographies, located in a social context (see for example Sikes *et al.* 1985; Cortazzi 1991; Goodson 1992; Huberman *et al.* 1993; Munro 1998; Weiler and Middleton 1999), and have utilized biographical narrative approaches to give meaning and temporal quality to the work, career and identity of the teacher. The teacher's work has increasingly come to be seen as biographically, as well as organizationally and socially, structured. Such studies have revealed the identity work which teachers routinely engage in through their everyday work and teaching experiences (Kehily 1995; Fenwick 1998). The experiences and identity work of students and pupils have also been explored, through a series of qualitative studies (see for example Mac an Ghaill 1994; Fordham 1996; Proweller 1998; Haw 1998).

Goodson (1997) summarizes the features of a biographical, experiential approach to the study of educational actors. His work has mainly focused on teachers, but the principles he identifies (and which are summarized below) are equally applicable to pupils and students.

- *Respect for the (auto)biographical, and the teacher's (student's) voice.* This recognizes personal experiences and individual voices as valuable and insightful ways of understanding the everyday realities of education.
- *Understanding the relationships between teaching experience and the accounts of teachers.* This recognizes that teaching (as career, work, profession, life) is replete with stories and narratives, and these can help to reveal the complex and diverse experiences of teaching, and education more generally. The same case can be made between learning experiences and the accounts students give of schooling. Hence the relationships between experience and narrative is key to understanding the process, practices and realities of education.
- *Recognizing the importance of life experiences and backgrounds to the everyday practice of teaching.* The lives and biographies of teachers cannot be separated from the work that they do. A life history, narrative approach ensures that teachers' backgrounds and experiences are treated seriously. It is also imperative that the everyday realities of schooling more generally are grounded in their social and cultural, and historical contexts.
- *Understanding the relationships between the teachers' lifestyles, latent identities and cultures.* Identities are complex, fragmented and shaped by understandings of lifestyle and culture. Gathering teacher narratives can help to make sense of the complexity of teacher-identity construction and teacher culture. Similarly student and pupil experiences and testimonies

can aid an understanding of student cultures and the identity-constructing processes in which young people are routinely engaged.

- *Recognizing the importance of lifecycle for the perceptions and practice of teaching.* A biographical, life history approach is sensitive to the relationships between the everyday realities of teaching and parameters such as age and generation, social status and parenthood. Here similar attendant claims can also be made for other social actors in the education system (especially so in the contemporary context of lifelong learning).
- *Documenting the importance of decisions and critical incidents.* Narratives and stories, collected through a biographical approach to educational processes, provide conventions and frameworks for articulating and making sense of careers, experiences and the construction of identity. They enable the identification of key figures, incidents, turning points and epiphanies (Denzin 1989) and thus enable the charting of decisions and progressions. This is especially important if we are to make sense of educational careers in their organizational and social context.

Goodson has been a key figure in proposing and utilizing a life history, biographical approach to the understanding of teachers' lives and educational processes. He sees an important place for the articulation of the identity work, and the biographical negotiation in which social actors are routinely engaged, in a grounded analysis of the everyday realities of education and schooling. But Goodson also reminds us of the structural value of studying individual lives and experiences. That is ensuring that personal narratives, individual lives and experiences are located within the situated, political and local contexts of education and schools. Simply to follow a postmodernist perspective of multiple, negotiated, free-floating selves ignores what Goodson (1997: 150) describes as 'the circumscribed spaces and socialised trajectories' of teachers' lives; a reminder that strategies for self-formation therefore take place in juxtaposition to the institutionalized and socialized practices of schooling. Identity and biographical work of educational social actors is both individual and structural.

This chapter now turns to a consideration of some of the ways in which students and teachers are engaged in identity construction and negotiation in educational contexts. This highlights the ways in which a concern with the biographical and identity work of educational actors can prove fruitful in understanding contemporary educational settings, experiences and social processes. What follows is not an exhaustive or systematic review, but rather an attempt to draw on a growing body of work which identifies the centrality of individual experiences as mechanisms for illuminating social processes in educational settings. Hence a focus is on the identity work with which social actors routinely engage in educational contexts, and how they articulate and make sense of these experiences.

Gendered identities

The gendered contexts of educational experiences, and the 'gender work' of schooling, have been increasingly recognized and documented. Sociological interest in gender and education has encompassed a wide range of issues, including issues of access and opportunity, policy and performance (Arnot *et al.* 1999; Salisbury and Riddell 1999), as well as the construction and re-production of masculinities and femininities (Mac an Ghaill 1994; Paechter 1998; Proweller 1998). A useful distinction can be made between a focus on the gendered *outcomes* of education, in terms of performance, career oppor-tunities, choices and trajectories, and the gendered *contexts* and *experiences* of school and educational processes. Early feminist concerns of girls' limited edu-cational access, opportunity and choice and educational under-performance have to some extent been superseded by contemporary concerns about the performance of boys and young men (see Arnot *et al.* 1998, 1999; Skelton 1998; Gorard *et al.* 1999; Raphael Reed 1999). Similarly, early work on the gendered contexts of social processes – especially in terms of the ways in which society reproduces certain kinds of stereotypical femininity and mas-culinity – no longer provides an adequate enough analysis of the ways in which 'gender' is constructed, created, negotiated and reproduced in educa-tional arenas. We now have a much more sophisticated and complicated understanding of the ways in which educational settings provide space and context for gender 'work' and the negotiated articulation of (gendered) identities (Weiner 1994; Haw 1998). Proweller (1998), for example, high-lights the multiple and shifting identities with which young people are now engaged. Drawing on her research of girls' experiences in private single sex schooling she argues that:

> it is no longer possible to speak of identity as constituted in one-to-one correspondence with the logic of school culture and society. Borders of self-definition are unclear as students living in the midst of the post-modern condition struggle daily to build lives with and against a sexy, hyper-saturated and mediated culture. Mapping their way towards self-definition involves continuous negotiation of the lived contradictions that class, race, ethnicity, sexuality and gender present against a challeng-ing urban backdrop.
>
> (Proweller 1998: 13)

It is impossible to attribute this increased understanding and articulation of the gendered identities of schooling to any one theoretical perspective or empirical trend. By means of illustration and illumination, two aspects are considered here. First, developments in educational feminist thinking are explored as a way of mapping increasingly complex articulations of gendered identities. Second, contemporary empirical interest in the relationships be-tween masculinities and schooling provide alternative discourses of identity formation in educational arenas.

Feminist educational thinking

Feminist scholars have been engaged in lengthy debate over the meanings of postmodernism (and post-structuralism) for feminist scholarship (see Weiner 1994; Haw 1998; Coffey and Delamont 2000 for useful summaries). What is clear is that feminism cannot ignore postmodernism. Some feminist commentators (see for example Fox-Genovese 1986; Brodribb 1992; Hoff 1994) have argued that postmodern theory challenges feminist research and theory to the point that it is politically paralysing and 'the cultural capital of late patriarchy' (Brodribb 1992: 78). Others offer a less sceptical interpretation, arguing for a more empowering vision of postmodernism (Flax 1993), or an understanding that postmodernism is not only compatible with the goals of feminism, but draws on perspectives already enshrined in contemporary feminist thought:

> I *do* believe that feminist theory has been immensely important in asking questions about knowledge, power, nature and wish it were more acknowledged that feminists were way ahead of postmodernists in critiquing the structures and universals of modernity.
>
> (Weiner 1994: 24, her emphasis)

Contemporary feminism encapsulates a range of feminist epistemologies, in keeping with a postmodern position, and an increasing concern with multiple subjectivities, roles and realities. There is a case to be made that feminism has always enshrined a range of theoretical positions and epistemologies, although this is not always acknowledged in historical narratives (Banks 1981). Contemporary understandings of the diversity of feminist thinking avoids any one form of feminism being set up as a dominant discourse and recognizes multiple narratives, meanings, realities and selves (Benhabib 1995). Recent articulations of this feminist position in educational contexts draw on the ideas of Foucault and post-structural perspectives to illuminate the importance of discursive practices and spaces to the formation of gendered identities (see for example Weiner 1994; Middleton 1995; Munro 1998; Blackmore 1999). These perspectives acknowledge the reality of multiple feminisms and identify the ways by which gender, power, difference, subject and agency are all constituted, though not determined, by discourse. Discursive practices 'constrain and shape possibilities for action, and therefore have the capacity to be both emancipating and repressive' (Blackmore 1999: 17). Post-structural feminism hence creates 'new ways of seeing and knowing' (Weiner 1994: 63), viewing social relations in terms of plurality and diversity, and recognizing that individuals are active in engaging in discourses through which they in turn are shaped.

This focus on the ways in which gender is constructed through discursive practices and reproduced in discursive spaces has led to educational research and scholarship concerned with the complexities, rather than any simple understanding, of (gender) identity formation and power relations. Thus women are no longer constructed as power*less*, and men as power*ful*. Rather gender is constructed and reconstructed in the discursive and social practices of educational arenas. Individuals can be (simultaneously) powerful and powerless in different discursive spaces (Blackmore 1999). Gender is dynamic, shifting and contradictory, and its relationship to power and authority equally so. Hence there has been an increasing empirical and theoretical concern with exploring how individuals negotiate discursive spaces and engage in fluid constructions of gendered identities. Of course, there is the potential inherent in such a position that gender is constantly viewed as 'in trouble' and in a constant state of (re)production and (re)creation. This can in turn make it difficult to develop theories of gender and power, and has the potential to render praxis and pedagogy based on such theories and understandings problematic. However, post-structuralist feminist perspectives have value in the ways in which they prioritize discursive and social practices that construct everyday educational life, and establish the contradictory natures of power and authority. This framework is drawn upon by Haw and her collaborators (1998) in an exploration of the educational experiences of Muslim girls in two schools in England. Drawing on post-structuralist feminism meant that

> the educational experiences of the Muslim students and their teachers in each school could be seen as a set of discursive relationships (discursive fields) consisting of a number of different and *sometimes* contradictory discourses, such as those of 'race', gender, class, culture and religion. Further, each of these discourses can themselves be considered as a discursive field, consisting of its own different discourses. Impacting on these discourses are other discourses to do with, for example, age, competence, physical ability and sexuality.
>
> (Haw 1998: 31)

Haw presents an empirical and theoretical project that locates the discursive positioning of Muslim students and their teachers (Muslim and non-Muslim). Distinguishing between primary and secondary discourses ('framing' and 'fleshing' discourses), Haw is able to chart how discourses shift and change as individuals negotiate discursive spaces and articulate complex (gendered, racialized) identities in the context of the school. This is an approach that is also utilized by Proweller (1998) in her ethnographic study of an elite, single sex private girls' school in the USA. Proweller mapped the identity formation processes that young women were engaged in through the processes and practices of education. She reappropriated the term 'borderland' (formerly used by post-colonial feminists to write about negotiating identities on the boundary of European and American culture) to 'describe the active repositioning of identities inside a school site of structural dominance' (1998: 13). Proweller explored the sometime contradictory discourses of race, class and gender in the context of this white, privileged, feminine setting, and considered how female identities are created and (re)constructed in these 'multiple borderlands'. She argued that these female school students were actively engaged in reconstituting their (class, race, gender) identities. For example, 'class identity production surfaces as a highly differentiated process that reminds us that identities are constructed across multiple discourses and practices that *have not* escaped the private school . . . students shape complicated processes of identity practice in the borderlands' (Proweller 1998: 93, her emphasis). Work such as that of Haw and Proweller, situated within contemporary articulations of feminist educational thinking, enable the notion of identity work to be regarded as a complicated set of social processes, whereby social actors (students, teachers) are actively involved in negotiating discursive spaces. These ideas are followed through in contemporary educational thinking and empirical work on masculinities and schooling.

Masculinity and identity

A case could be made that contemporary work on boys, masculinity and schooling has resulted in the 'reappropriation' of educational agendas by men and patriarchy (see Skelton 1998 for a summary of recent work on masculinities and men's studies). While that may be viewed as a somewhat uncharitable position, there is little doubt that masculinities and the construction of male gendered identities have become an increasing focus for research and theoretical work on gender, identity construction and education. There have certainly been cautionary warnings from some feminists, and indeed some men working in the field, that such work should not romanticize or privilege boys and men within education, nor render the feminist project in education redundant (Cannan and Griffin 1990; Skelton 1998; Lingard and Douglas 1999). For our purposes here it is important to stress that the increased empirical and theoretical work on masculinities in education, undertaken by both male and female scholars, has been hugely important in furthering our understanding of the gendered identity 'work' of boys and girls, men and women. It should come as no surprise that feminists have increasingly been among the main researchers of masculinities in school, and that key areas of debate for feminists in educational research have informed the agenda for studying masculinities and schooling – for example in examining the sexual politics of the classroom and exploring 'how discourses of racism, gender, sexuality and class articulate within specific contexts to inform the formation of masculine identities' (Skelton 1998: 221; see also Thorne 1993; Connolly 1995; Mac an Ghaill 1994; Epstein *et al.* 1998 and Raphael Reed 1999).

Empirical and theoretical work on masculinities has informed our understandings of the ways in which educational arenas offer constructions and interpretations of gendered identities, and the ways in which some masculinities (and femininities) can be legitimated, challenged or redefined as *Other* (Paechter 1998). More generally such work has brought to the fore the negotiated practices which shape (gendered) identities. Haywood and Mac an Ghaill (1996), for example, considered the ways in which schools shape masculinities. This builds on the earlier well-cited work of Mac an Ghaill (1994) on the formation and interpretation of masculinities in an English secondary school. Haywood and Mac an Ghaill identified a number of school factors that contributed to the construction and reproduction of masculine identities. These included the use of certain kinds of disciplinary procedures and tactics, the use of language, the curriculum and attendant stratification of knowledge, and the implicit and explicit organization of sexuality within school processes. Hence there are 'particular spaces where "masculinity-making" appears both explicit and abundant' (Haywood and Mac an Ghaill 1996: 52). Schools serve as sites where different styles of masculinities are (re)produced and used. Schools do not produce these masculine identities in isolation, but interrelate with other social and cultural sites. Schooling is a particularly strategic site of identity work,

> as it offers a condensed range of experiences in a sustained and mandatory fashion. It is also necessary to emphasize that schools do not produce masculinities in a direct, overly deterministic way, but that

> the construction of students' identities is a process of negotiation, re-
> jection, acceptance and ambivalence.
>
> (Haywood and Mac an Ghaill 1996: 59)

The study of masculinities in schools has contributed to our understandings
of the ways in which gendered identities are constructed and reproduced,
and to the notion that *masculinity* can take many forms and has many
interpretations – some of which are legitimized, others stigmatized, others
challenged (Kenway 1995). Hence the school is highlighted as a significant
site for the gendered identity work of students, and indeed teachers (see
Sumison 1999; Whitehead 1998; Coffey and Delamont 2000). In the next section sexuality is considered, as a further factor in the formation of identities
in educational settings.

Sexualities and schooling

Lesbian and gay students and teachers have not been the subject of wide
sociological investigation. Work that has been done, however, provides a
particularly good illustration of the identity and biographical work that is so
central to the educational experience. Lesbian and gay teachers, for example,
have been revealed as managing their identity in often trying circumstances
and social contexts, regularly exposed to homophobia, heterosexism and
hostility. Their teacher identity has been shown to be compounded and
mediated by their sexuality (Scott 1989; Griffin 1991; Khayatt 1992; Epstein
1994; Clarke 1996). Ferfolja's (1998) study of the sexual harassment experiences of Australian lesbian teachers is illustrative of this. Using in-depth
interviews with lesbian teachers, Ferfolja explored how homophobia and
sexual harassment was an integral part of their lives: 'the effects of the
harassment were stressful for all of the teachers. However for some, the
experience was disabling' (Ferfolja 1998: 405).

The relationships between the public (teaching) life/identity and the
personal (lesbian) life/identity are complex. (Auto)biographical accounts
reveal that 'coming out' at school can be fraught with difficulties, and that
many lesbian teachers adopt 'passing strategies' in order to keep their lesbian
identity from their colleagues and students (Squirrell 1989; Epstein 1994;
Sparkes 1994; Clarke 1996; Khayatt 1997). In (re)presenting his life history
interviews with Jessica, a lesbian physical education teacher in England,
Sparkes (1994) notes the ways in which Jessica felt the need to separate her
personal and professional life. Resigned to the patriarchal (and heterosexual)
cultural rules and resources that shape interactions in the staffroom,

> [Jessica's] identity management strategy is framed within the 'profes-
> sional' expectation held by many of her colleagues, that one's private
> home life should be kept separate from one's public work life. In par-
> ticular, issues of sexual identity are commonly assumed to be 'private'
> affairs that should not be brought into the public and professional
> world of work.
>
> (Sparkes 1994: 111)

Jessica's enforced silence about her sexuality made her question her ability to teach, and left her unable to challenge sexism in the staffroom and classroom. Clarke's (1996) in-depth interviews with lesbian physical education student teachers and qualified teachers in England revealed similar tensions. Clarke noted that the subject matter of physical education – and the centrality of the body to that – exacerbates the identity management issues for lesbian PE teachers. Clarke (1996) documents how lesbian teacher identities are often construed and shaped by heterosexual others (see Paechter 1998). Lesbian teachers often straddle the dual identities of lesbian and pseudo-heterosexual. In concealing their lesbian identities from colleagues and pupils, these lesbian teachers employed mechanisms and strategies to 'cover tracks' and deflect attention from their sexual identity. Staffroom conversations were managed to minimize discussions of home life and partners, intimate friendships with school colleagues were avoided, as were general conversations about homosexuality. Homophobic and heterosexist comments were not challenged – but rather endured for fear of 'drawing attention'. Some also adopted strategies to put colleagues 'off the scent' – being overly flirtatious with male colleagues, for example. These staffroom strategies carried over into the everyday realities and interactions of the classroom. These lesbian teachers were ambiguous in discussions about 'significant' others, and where possible (within the particular confines of the physical nature of their subject) avoided physical contact and situations which might be perceived as having pseudo-sexual connotations. Clarke counters the negativity of her accounts of these lesbian teachers' experiences with the observation that successful 'passing' as a pseudo-heterosexual can be perceived as a form of active resistance; 'getting away with it becomes a means of resisting and challenging, albeit in perhaps a rather hidden way; this too is another paradox of their identities' (Clarke 1996: 205). (It is worth noting here that pupil folklore and stories are replete with tales of the lesbian or gay physical education teacher and the attendant concerns of the body. The identity management issues of the lesbian teacher are hence compounded by fears and concerns of the predatory lesbian teacher – see, for example, Pugsley *et al.* 1996; Paechter 1998.)

Unlike the lesbian teachers interviewed by Clarke, some do 'choose' to reveal their lesbian identity, coming out to colleagues and students (see Beck 1994; Klages 1994; Wright 1998). Adams and Emery (1994) share anecdotes and strategies of classroom coming out stories and provide advice on ways and means. They locate coming out in a broader context of creating an open and safe classroom space – in which coming out is part of the process; a moment rather than an end. Blinick (1994) provides an autobiographical account of coming out – and how she prepared for the day, including choosing what to wear (a frilly dress and pearls) and how to wear her hair (loose and on her shoulders). She highlights a position – which will have resonance among many other women (black/(dis)abled) teachers – of how she found herself being extra good and extra dedicated (a kind of super-teacher) in order to prove how wonderful lesbian teachers are! She also relates coming out to the more general issue of providing role models and teaching sexuality in the classroom. She felt she had a responsibility to come out. 'I felt it was crucial for young people – especially those questioning their sexual orientation or who already knew they were lesbian, gay, or bisexual – to see another healthy, happy and productive lesbian' (Blinick 1994: 143). This is an issue which Clarke (1996: 204) also addressed – not only were the lesbian teachers she talked to 'forced to suffer in silence but pupils are also denied the opportunity for lesbian role models'. Wright (1998) presents her coming out story in such a context – as one strategy for fighting homophobia and heterosexism in the classroom, providing a dialogue which can be simultaneously empowering and difficult, even frightening. In commenting on her autobiographical narrative, Wright underlines this balance and interweaving of the personal and the professional:

> I am more aware now than I was when I originally wrote this article of the emotional toll that coming out in the classroom takes on me. In this article I emphasise the positive effects of coming out both on myself and on my students – who so clearly benefited from authenticity. I remain convinced that the benefits outweighed the costs for me, as well. However, I am struck and challenged by the fact that it hasn't gotten any easier for me over the years and that the initial experience of coming out still leaves me feeling raw and vulnerable.
>
> (Wright 1998: 191)

Lesbian and gay students face similar identity management issues (see Epstein 1994, 1997; Mac an Ghaill 1994; Epstein and Johnson 1998). These are integrally linked to masculine and feminine identities, and to legitimate versions of masculinity and femininity. Epstein's (1997) interviews with boys who had been 'cissies' at school revealed the lack of support these young people had, as they were engaged in the production and construction of their gendered and sexualized identities. The need for support from other gay men and boys was a particularly pertinent issue, as one boy indicated:

> There was absolutely nobody I could go to . . . You can't sit down and talk to somebody who, about, you know, specifically issues around coming out, around having boyfriends, trouble with that, about whether you're gay or not, if that person isn't themselves . . . I know friends of mine who, you know, reached that stage, that fatal age of fifteen or sixteen, decided to come out, had no support at all and were completely scared by it.
>
> (Epstein 1997: 110–11)

A focus on sexuality and sexual identity can reveal complex ways in which the identity work is engaged with, negotiated and enacted in educational contexts. While I have chosen here to focus on homosexual and in particular lesbian identity construction, there are other aspects that could be followed up and explored, for example expectations of sexuality and the formation of the heterosexual identity (Jones and Mahony 1989; Epstein and Johnson 1998; Morris and Fuller 1999), or the relationship between the school, identity work and the body. Commentators have revealed the ways in which schooling and educational processes are embodied, and the ways in which the body is controlled, legitimated, regulated and managed in educational contexts (see

Holland *et al.* 1991; Delamont 1998; Epstein and Johnson 1998; Welland 1998). Hence we should also be aware of the ways in which the body inter-relates to other biographical work we are routinely engaged in (Coffey 1999).

Race and identity

The relationship between race and education has a long history. Educationalists have been a long-established professional group engaged in the struggle against racism. This has taken on new understandings and meanings in late 1990s Britain where, for example, the contemporary concern with nationhood and Britishness has refocused the role of ethnic minority groups in relation to an imaginary (white) homogeneous Britain (Gillborn 1998). Sociologists of education concerned with issues of race have been concerned to reveal the ways in which the education system operates in racialized ways – whether discriminatory or otherwise. There has been a long tradition of quantitative research in this area, which has attempted to quantify how minority students perform in education (Smith and Tomlinson 1989), and conclusions have been mixed. Critiques of such approaches have, like similar approaches to gender, argued that they do not go far enough in articulating the multiple and complex ways in which race and racism construct and reconstruct the identities of students in their everyday social (and school) lives. Qualitative studies over the last two decades or so have attempted to chart the realities of life in schools, and the concurrent aspects of identity work that young people are engaged in, taking race and ethnicity as a central feature of the analysis. Mac an Ghaill's research in English secondary schools is a particu-larly good example of this approach (1988; see also Mac an Ghaill 1994).

Mac an Ghaill utilized the concepts of accommodation and resistance to chart the strategies by which ethnic minority students constructed and established their identities in educational arenas. In *Young, Gifted and Black* (1988) Mac an Ghaill identified groups of students actively engaged in man-aging and reproducing racialized and ethnic identities. For example, the 'Black Sisters' valued the acquisition of educational qualifications, while be-ing acutely aware of the discriminatory practices of race and gender within the school. A group of Asian and African-Caribbean sixth form female stu-dents of an inner city sixth form college, engaged in subtle forms of resistance in the school context (arriving late, completing homework late, remaining silent in any group 'discussions', talking in *other* languages rather than schoolroom English). They were sympathetic to those students who adopted more vigorous antisocial tactics but challenged notions that they should not value education. They devised ways of ensuring positive identities, maintaining collective solidarity while doing well in school, but at the same time internally rejecting the racialized contexts of everyday school life.

Mac an Ghaill (1988) also identified sub-groups of male students who utilized forms of resistance to maintain and construct identities in the face of the perceived racialization of the school context. The 'Warriors', a group of working-class Asian boys, adopted covert antisocial practices – conversing in their first language, 'explained' absenteeism, and collectivity in the classroom – as mechanisms for maintaining a sense of collective identity. Many of these mechanisms remained largely invisible to teachers, but enabled the students actively to manage and maintain their ethnic identities. In contrast, the 'Rasta Heads', a group of African-Caribbean boys in a comprehensive school, were highly visible in the ways in which they negotiated their racialized identities. Their overt rejection of schooling, articulated by language, dress, refusals, rejection of school rules and routines, could be perceived as challenging the intellectual and social (white) hegemony and as active resistance to racist structures. Mac an Ghaill returns to the relationship between race, identity and schooling in his later work (1994), exploring how they interact with sexuality and masculinity.

Fordham (1996) in an ethnographic study of a high school in Washington DC, USA, provides useful analytical purchase on these relationships between schooling, race and the formation of identity. Fordham looked at how African-American students coped with and accommodated school. She argues that both high achievement and low achievement brought strategies for establishing and maintaining a black cultural identity in the school setting. School achievers and failures adopted different yet comparable strategies to resist school and maintain their black identity. The high achievers outwardly conformed to the norms and values of academic success. Fordham argues that conformity in and of itself was a form of active resistance. High achievers actively worked to disprove what Fordham calls 'black lack'. They defined their black identity in terms of academically succeeding, thereby disproving perceptions of low black achievement. In comparison, low achievers rejected the positive claims of schooling. Their various strategies of resistance and techniques of avoidance are conceptualized by Fordham as a refusal to 'act white'. Oppositional rather than conformist strategies were used to achieve positive black identities. Fordham terms this a refusal to liquidate the self: 'Liquidating the black self is vigorously resisted . . . most of these students view success in school as embodying the construction of otherness, and they associate such success with an inevitable degree of self alienation' (Fordham 1996: 283). Other commentators, such as Proweller (1998) and Haw (1998), have undertaken the task of revealing the ways in which racialized identities are mediated at school by other identities such as social status, class, gender, religion and culture. The study by Haw on the education of Muslim girls in the British context reveals how such discourses articulate in the social construction of their identity(-ies). Proweller adopted broad conceptualizations of racialized identity production by considering the narrated experiences of both white and black students in an arena of private schooling. In doing so, Proweller (1998: 96) complicates understandings of the relationships between 'race', identity and educational contexts, not least by examining 'whiteness as a fractured and continuously shifting racial border'.

Conclusion

This chapter has sought to explore some of the relationships between identity, biography and education. As the self has become an increasing focus of contemporary sociology, and as biography and narrative have become increasingly important aspects of empirical work in education, it is vital that we constitute and reveal schooling as a site for the identity work of students and teachers. Educational processes and practices provide ongoing locations for the negotiation, (re)production and (re)presentation of selves in contemporary society. The concept of 'identity work' (or biographical work) captures the experiential formulation of education, and allows an analysis of the interactions between individual social actors and particular educational settings. It moves us away from simple equations of powerfulness and powerlessness and allows for a broader conceptualization, revealing the ways in which individual identities are shaped by collective experiences and structural processes. Hence personal narratives (and biographizing the social) have value, in terms of both documenting the everyday realities of educational (school) life and understanding these realities in shifting theoretical, educational and social times.

The next chapter focuses on the differential routes through, and outcomes of, contemporary educational experiences, and draws on similar analytical ideas to this chapter, for example the ways in which experiences of education are multiple and complex, and the ways in which these are mediated by social factors, such as class and gender. Whereas this chapter began with the value of individual experiences in being able to reveal and make sense of social processes, the following chapter adopts a more 'top-down' approach. It considers the relationship between education, economy and society, and how this maps onto the desirability and realities of educational pathways and results.

6 Pathways, outcomes *and* difference

Introduction

A recurrent theme in literatures on sociology of education is the differential outcomes of education in terms of achievement and performance. This reflects a long-standing concern with documenting the successes and failures of education systems. Early work in this area tended to concentrate primarily on social class differentials in educational achievement, linking these to consequent labour market positions. Hence, the sociology of education has made a substantial contribution to classic work on social class and social mobility, through charting the class patterns of educational provision and educational outcomes. Exploring the relationships between social class and schooling highlights the more general linkages between the labour market, and the economy, society, social justice, and education. While social class remains central to explorations of social inequality and education, contemporary work has highlighted the ways in which educational outcomes and inequalities are also gendered, racialized and sexualized, as well as class-based. Moreover, it has increasingly been recognized that simply to conceptualize educational outcomes in terms of measurable scores (such as examination performance or labour market destination) denies the complex realities of educational experiences. Hence there has been an increasing focus on the cultural reproduction of difference and the politics of identity construction that occurs in and through the process of schooling, and education more generally. The routes that individuals and social groups navigate through the education system, and the outcomes of those educational experiences, are now recognized as much more complex and multifaceted than early work perhaps suggested.

This chapter focuses on the differential conceptualizations of educational outcome. The 'end products', or potential outcomes, of education are located within contemporary educational processes and societal shifts. The chapter is divided into four main sections, the first of which outlines some of the historical and contemporary relationships between economy, society and education. In mapping the shifts in the economy and labour market needs, this section considers the ways in which educational aims and outcomes

are interwoven with economic change. In turn, sociological work on education has always attempted to document how the outcomes of education
have social, as well as economic, consequences and opportunities attached
to them. Hence this section also considers the social justice possibilities and/
or realities of education. The second section of this chapter addresses alternative conceptualizations and understandings of educational outcomes. In
particular the section documents some of the sociological shifts away from
simple considerations of social class, and indeed away from conceptualizing
outcome in simple comparative (and largely quantitative) terms. The notions
of difference and identity construction are introduced as alternative ways of
making sense of educational outcomes. Ironically, these more holistic interpretations of educational outcome stand in sharp contrast to contemporary
educational–political aims of increasingly assessing schools and students
through the accumulation of explicit measures such as examination and
assessment performance (via for example the publication of school league
tables; see Chapter 2 of this volume). The last two substantial sections of the
chapter draw on recent 'outcome' debates. The first of these reconsiders
issues of achievement and performance in the light of contemporary concerns over the education of boys. The second addresses broader social outcomes of education, by focusing on the area of citizenship education.

Education, economy and society

The outcomes of education have been most vigorously contextualized in
terms of the relationships between education, the economy and society.
These relationships are both long-standing and well founded, particularly in
terms of the ways in which education is thought to contribute to both
economic prosperity and social justice. The recognition and assessment of
these linkages have paved the way for a sociology of education embedded in
documenting and exploring the pathways and outcomes of education. This
has explored how both individuals and social groups make their way through
the education system *and* how their experience of education contributes to
labour market, and to economic and social outcomes. Commentators have
noted the fluidity and shifting nature of these relationships during the second
half of the twentieth century, from the postwar period of economic growth to
more uncertain times at the turn of the new century (see Brown *et al.* 1997).
The sustained period of economic growth in the postwar period firmly
located the role of education within the political economy of nations. This
period of economic nationalism with its triple pillars of prosperity, security
and opportunity established the route of social progress through sustained
national economic growth. Here, education was firmly woven into the fabric
of economic life, and seen as vital to the development and maintenance of
advanced industrial societies. Moreover, education was viewed during this
period with considerable optimism. The expansion of, and increased opportunities offered by, education enabled the articulation of meritocratic principles
and more generally social justice, bound together as foundation stones of
economic stability *and* a democratic society. The development of a postwar

sociology of education was charged with documenting these educational processes. Commentators were keen to establish and map the emergent relationships between state education, national economies and the wider society. Research focused upon issues of access and the expansion and widening of educational opportunities. The actual and potential roles of education in social mobility and the pursuit of the meritocratic ideal were systematically explored and documented.

The last quarter of the twentieth century saw significant shifts, both to the established relationships between education, society and the economy *and* in the emphasis and preoccupations of the sociology of education as an empirical discipline. These shifts are interrelated, although they are not necessarily mirror images of one another. Indeed there has been divergence as well as convergence over the emphases adopted by the state education system, and the emergent concerns of the sociology of education at the end of the twentieth century. Educational policy and governance have sought to re-establish and redefine the relationships between education, economy and society during a period of economic and social change. Sociological research over a similar period has continued to document shifting relationships, but has also been concerned with revealing the differentiated and multiple educational experiences, and exploring the range of identities which are supported, acknowledged and legitimated by such experiences.

Economic recessions of the 1970s and 1980s, usually traced to international crises of the early 1970s, undermined the postwar ideals of economic prosperity and secure nationalism. In the wake of this came uncertain economic and occupational futures, and changing labour markets. The relationship between education and economic productivity, always a difficult relationship to chart empirically, became ever more questionable in the face of shifting and increasing difficult economic times. At the same time educationalists, sociologists and politicians began to question the implicit and assumed role of education in seeking to bring about social justice, equality and a democratic society. State education was increasingly challenged from all sides of the political spectrum, accused of failing in terms of both its economic and social mandates. Education was no longer meeting the needs of a changing economy and redefined labour market (although of course some would question whether these were ever wholly realistic goals for an education system). Educational failure was also perceived in terms of the educational outcomes of certain individuals and social groups. Educational opportunities had not been sufficiently expansive as to eradicate inequalities and social divisions. The principle of meritocracy, on which education in advanced industrial societies was founded, came to be seen as increasingly flawed. As Brown *et al.* (1997: 13) note, 'meritocratic competition has been a means of legitimating occupational and social inequalities because the doctrine of meritocracy is based on giving everyone an equal chance to be unequal'.

There have been shifts in the relationships between society, the economy and education, mediated by the state. The perceived power and ability of education to deliver the needs of the economy has not been fundamentally challenged, but has shifted to accommodate perceived new economic needs. Education has still remained as a core element of any aims to achieve economic renewal. There has continued to be a concern with increasing the absolute opportunities for education, while the scope of education has been explicitly extended to provide more access, more (and diverse) educational routes and more training opportunities. This has been coupled with an increased diversification and selection process – channelling individuals into certain kinds of educational experiences means re-establishing the links between education and economic life. The role of training and education has arguably become more, rather than less, central to the labour market. Certification of skills and increased emphasis on credentialization have become key to understanding the measurable aims and outcomes of education. Hence the *outcomes* of education have remained at the heart of the relationship between education and economy. The nature and teaching of skills has also shifted in emphasis. There has always been a tension between general and technical education, or between social and vocational skills. The changing nature of the economy, and the post-industrial emphasis on a flexible workforce, has exacerbated this tension, increasing the desirability of furnishing young people with social and personal skills, appropriate for their labour market futures. Hence the role of formal education has become increasingly defined in terms of the balance between the vocational skills (increasingly provided in post-compulsory and on-the-job educational settings) and the skills and personal qualities necessary for successful participation in contemporary economic (and social) life.

It is possible to understand the changing nature of education and its shifting relationship to economy and society in contrastive ways. The increased opportunities for educational participation (exemplified in the concept of lifelong learning) can be conceptualized as part of a movement toward a learning society and attendant discourses of social justice and democracy. In such an interpretation, certification serves as a mechanism for documenting equality of opportunity and outcome. Similarly, recent moves toward the formal inclusion of social, personal and 'citizen' skills in the school and post-compulsory curriculum can also be interpreted as significant routes towards democratic citizenship. Hence the ideals of democracy, social justice and the active citizen become sustained within the new rhetorics of education (such as certification, credentialization and citizenship education). An alternative interpretation of this scenario can also be offered. The shifting emphases of education and the redefining of its links to economy and society re-establishes long-held understandings of the role of education as a function of social control. The increased emphasis on the role of education in the formation of citizenship, and the extension of education and training throughout a lifetime, can be conceptualized in terms of surveillance and discipline of the individual.

The changing nature of contemporary education, and its assumed links to economic and social ambitions, has been paralleled by the shifting parameters of the sociological investigation of education. The changing educational and policy climate has led to sociological investigation which is largely policy driven (Ball 1990; Edwards 1990; Ozga 2000), concerned with charting the process, progress and consequences of significant educational reform (see Chapter 8). At the same time there has been a sustained increase of interest in the accounts and narratives of educational experience. Sociologists of education have also remained committed to understanding the process of education in terms of relationships to economy and society. However, the ways in which these are construed have been subject to some shift. Rather than concentrating solely on measurable issues of access, selection and outcome, there have been moves towards understanding the complexities of the relationships and processes of education (and its attendant links to economic and social issues). Hence, there has been a move away from attempting to chart educational outcomes without significant attention to the processes by which those outcomes are reached. Notions of equality and *inequality* have been compounded by considerations of knowledge and pedagogy on the one hand, and cultural politics and difference on the other. The connotations of opportunities and outcomes (played out in terms of equality and inequality) have been counterbalanced by sociological conceptualizations of educational experiences and processes. Hence attempts have increasingly been made to explore and articulate the cultural politics of education and difference.

Of course, these alternative discourses are only in part due to the changing nature of education *per se,* and are linked to broader changes in intellectual and social life. The abandoning of grand theories, and the increasing concern with how selves are constructed through cultural practices, are major tenets of a postmodernist agenda (Lash and Urry 1987; Lyotard 1992; Hall and Jacques 1989). For some sociologists of education this has translated into a need to understand, make visible and make sense of complex relationships between education, economy and society, at the level of both individuals and social groups. Hence newly established interest in the formation of identities has been matched by the rethinking of the interrelationships between class, gender, ethnicity and education. At the heart of this is one of the central dilemmas of contemporary education. That is whether education is really concerned with cultural reproduction (maintenance of the cultural status quo and inculcation of 'societal' values) or cultural interruption (changing the social order; providing the means to new identities and challenging the conventional outcomes of education). The shifts in the educational order, and the changes in the preoccupations of the sociology of education both pivot on the articulation of this problematic. That is, how education is utilized to meet the perceived needs of economy, state and society, and the ways in which this serves to reproduce or interrupt cultural practices. This chapter now moves on to consider this through an exploration of outcomes and differences which are mediated through contemporary educational processes and practices.

Outcomes and/or difference

The relationship between social class differentials and education outcome has been a central and recurrent concern of the sociology of education. Indeed, class has been linked to education throughout the twentieth century, from early concerns with increasing education in order to educate (or control?)

the working-class masses, through postwar concerns with increased social mobility and meritocracy, to contemporary worries over insecure economies and the need to guard against detrimental or downwards social mobility. Research in the postwar sociology of education took on board the idea and desire of social mobility and sought systematically to chart the role of education in terms of absolute and relative mobility, both within and between social classes. This work responded to the early political arithmetic model of social stratification and social mobility (Glass 1954), which ascertained that there had in fact been little in the way of sustained upward mobility. Later studies that articulated a more complex picture were also drawn upon, for example, the work of Goldthorpe and his colleagues (1980) who were able to document increases in absolute social mobility (we are all better off than we were) but little changes in relative mobility (class differentials remaining relatively robust). Sustained social commentary has problematized social class differentials, but recurrently concluded that they have remained – in spite of educational policies, which at least on the surface purported to have social mobility and social justice at their core. Significantly, from the perspective of educational outcomes, levels of educational achievement continue to be linked in systematic and demonstrable ways to socio-economic background (Bourdieu and Passerson 1977; Nash 1997, 1999). In terms of formal educational qualifications it has continued to be demonstrated that there is a systematic relationship between poor examination achievement and low social class (Denscombe 1994). Indeed, as Brown *et al.* (1997) note, poverty has remained central to the outcomes of education. And, of course, it is well documented that poverty intersects with social factors such as class, race and gender (Glendinning and Millar 1992; Hills 1995).

At the heart of discussions about the impact of education in changing the patterns of class and social mobility has been the social context of schooling. It remains a common assumption that in replicating the society of which it is a part, education is more explicitly involved in cultural reproduction than in cultural interruption. Given this stance, it is debatable whether schooling can ever be an effective means of change rather than simply a mechanism for maintaining the status quo (Burgess and Parker 1999). This raises fundamental questions about the role of education in the context of the state. Should education be concerned with social reproduction and social control, and what are the limitations and possibilities of a state education system to foreshadow social change? How far an education system can be a vehicle of social change remains a question of contention. Moreover, there are different understandings of desirable social change. There is, for example, a world of difference between espousing, say, social justice and enhanced democratic participation, and responding to the needs of an economy increasingly dependent upon diversification, credentialization and a flexible workforce.

Some commentators have argued that class has lost its central place in the sociology of education (see for example Mortimore and Whitty 1997). It is almost certainly the case that examining the role of education in sustaining a meritocracy and increasing social mobility is no longer (if it ever was) an especially productive way of approaching sociological studies of education. Simply equating education to notions of performance and academic achievement, and in turn to understandings of social class, simplifies the relationships between education, economy and society. However, the increased selection procedures, choice processes and diversification of schools are still fundamentally about social class, as Ball (1993) and Gewirtz *et al.* (1995) among others have demonstrated (see Chapter 3 and Chapter 8). Sociological work on school choice and the educational market place has broadly supported the view that recent educational reforms have served to maintain or exacerbate socio-economic differences, rather than significantly aid their eradication. The notion of choice has, albeit implicitly, replaced the concept of equality of opportunity in education; and this in turn has had consequences for the aspirations and realities of education to respond to socio-economic differentials.

Sociological work on education has not abandoned inequalities in education, but has broadened the ways in which the topic is approached. Rather than documenting the failure or success of schools in a kind of causal way, attention has increasingly been given over to the processes and relationships of education (Gewirtz *et al.* 1995). As educational audit (see Chapter 2) has increasingly demanded the explicit comparison of measurable performance indicators, sociological investigations of educational experiences have tried to move away from simple equations of educational success and failure, toward mapping the complexities of educational experiences and how these relate to the formation of complex identities. This shift has occurred partly as a response to increasingly complex ways of understanding social difference, not only in terms of class, but also (for example) in terms of race, sexuality, age and gender.

Contemporary understandings of gender and education have increasingly shifted away from the preoccupation with educational performance, although notably the recent debates over the supposed underperformance of boys, engaged in by academics, policy makers and the media, has reopened interest in gendered examination performances as measurable educational outcomes. These debates are examined in more detail later in this chapter (see Epstein *et al.* 1998 for a summary and discussions of these debates, and Gorard *et al.* 1999 who reanalyse the data that purport to demonstrate the underachievement of boys). Feminist educational scholars have increasingly challenged the ways in which knowledge and pedagogy are defined, and have revealed the hegemonic masculinities on which the foundations of education are built. These arguments are not confined to feminism, but have been reiterated by other feminist-informed research (see Mac an Ghaill 1994; Connell 1995; Skelton 1998; Lingard and Douglas 1999). Contemporary studies of gender and education have focused on the gendered regimes and relationships of educational process and praxis, and the ways in which these contribute to the formation and reproduction of identities in contemporary society (Blair and Holland 1995; Munro 1998; Proweller 1998; Coffey and Delamont 2000). Gender also complicates possible educational aims of social justice, equality, citizenship and democracy (see Arnot and Weiler 1993; Lister 1997; Arnot *et al.* 1999).

Similarly sociological research on race, ethnicity and education has (re-)established the relationships between cultural identity, educational performance and experience (see for example Mac an Ghaill 1988; Mirza 1992; Troyna 1993a; Gillborn 1995; Fordham 1996). Race and ethnicity are no longer conceptualized as factors that can impede or problematize educational performance in any simple causal way. It is still imperative to document the relative successes and failures of education in relation to 'race' and ethnicity. There is empirical evidence which continues to support the argument that some groups of students consistently do less well in formal school performance analyses (see Smith and Tomlinson 1989; Drew and Gray 1991; Pilkington 1999). But increasingly research has undertaken the task of understanding the variety of positions, experiences and ethnic identities open to, accepted, resisted and challenged by pupils and students.

Educational outcomes remain central to contemporary understandings of educational policy, process and practices. However, it is important to recognize that educational outcomes go beyond simple equations of externally measured performance (despite policy agendas and the use of comparative league tables which suggest the contrary). Changes to the economy, to society and to the ways of theorizing and understanding these, lead to redefinitions and re-examinations of the meanings, experiences and pathways of education. This has shifted sociological emphasis towards an understanding of education in terms of cultural politics and the documenting of difference. This approach encompasses some key themes such as

- *Knowledge and pedagogy.* Exploring what is taught and how, and the way in which these serve as mechanisms for understanding how education undertakes certain kinds of cultural reproduction. This makes explicit the relationships between knowledge, pedagogy and outcome, clearly linking curriculum and teaching with the processes of learning and the educational and cultural outcomes of schooling (see Chapter 4).
- *Processes of reproduction.* Education is considered as process, rather than simply as outcome. Hence schools are sites for cultural reproduction, and indeed potential sites for cultural interruption or change. Educational outcomes become redefined in terms of the (re)production of class, gendered, racialized and sexualized identities. A good example of this complexity would be considerations of gender and education. As well as understanding the gender processes of schooling in terms of measurable achievements, we can also address the role of schooling in the construction of certain kinds of masculine, feminine and sexual identities.
- *Exclusion and inclusion.* Attention has increasingly turned to the ways in which education is implicated in social exclusion and inclusion. This has ramifications for simple measures of outcome – in terms of labour market opportunities and credentialization – but also relates to broader conceptions of educational outcomes in terms of citizenship and social justice. Recent government announcements more firmly locating citizenship as part of the educational objective are fundamentally concerned with questions of exclusion and inclusion.
- *Power and control.* These concepts are still useful in articulating relationships between state, class and education. They also have mileage in articulating the everyday realities and experiences of education. The complexities of

these imply that the measurements of schooling are multiple and diverse, and not subjected to simple equations of performance, or ideological aims of social control. In interacting with the policies and practices of education, social actors experience power and powerlessness in interwoven ways (Paechter 1998). In implicitly participating in the politics of identity, learners (and indeed teachers) actively construct and shape their educational biographies. This does not deny the role of the state in shaping educational policy. But it does provide other mechanisms of accounting for and articulating diverse educational experiences.

These more complex understandings of educational outcome contribute to new vocabularies of identity and difference. To examine these further the following sections of this chapter explore some contemporary educational debates/issues that are fundamentally concerned with shaping the outcomes of education process, policy and practice. First the renewed and recast debates over gender and achievement are discussed. Second, the role of education in the transition to adulthood is explored by turning attention to recent moves in England to (re-)establish an education for citizenship in schools.

Rethinking gender and achievement

The 1990s saw a redirecting of interest in gender and educational achievement. Media, policy and scholarly interest specifically focused on the perceived educational underachievement of boys and young men. Evidence for the phenomenon of the 'underachieving boy' lies primarily with interpretations of measurable educational performances (such as formal assessments and examination grades). The relatively weaker performance of boys compared to girls has been claimed across most subject areas, although the range of the differential is not consistent for all subjects, and in one or two subject areas boys have been shown to outperform girls (Arnot *et al*. 1996, 1998, 1999). The trend has been particularly identified up to the age of 16 years (GCSE level in England and Wales), although supporting evidence is also apparent at further and higher education levels (Arnot *et al*. 1996; Speed 1998). Identified in the UK, it has also been claimed as something of an international or global phenomenon (Jackson 1998; Mahony 1998). Weis (1990) has identified the underachievement of boys (especially working-class boys) in the United States of America; similarly trends have been noted in Australia (see Mills and Lingard 1997) and the Caribbean (see Parry 1996). Mahony (1998: 46) places the current debate of underachieving boys into a broader, global context of change, arguing that 'the concern about boys fits into a wider set of issues about the relationship of the nation state to the global economy and into a range of anxieties concerned with reasserting patriarchal dominance'. The shifts toward international labour markets, the preoccupation with competitiveness and a global economy demanding new styles of educational management (Collinson and Hearn 1996; Coffey and Delamont 2000), together with concerns over safeguarding masculinity in the face of a changing social climate (Kruse 1996), have made the issue of achievement in general, and underperformance in particular, increasingly significant as an indicator of the efficiency and effectiveness of schooling.

As with all 'moral panics' or urban myths there are elements of 'truth' in these stories of male underachievement although, as many commentators have agreed, a simplistic interpretation of complex 'achievement' data fails to articulate the nuances and complexities of gender and achievement at the end of the twentieth century (Epstein *et al.* 1998; Delamont 1999, 2000; Raphael Reed 1999). Gorard *et al.* (1999) have argued that the gender gap in the performances of girls and boys has systematically been misunderstood. In their reanalysis of statutory assessments and examination results in Wales, they argue that the gap in favour of girls mainly appears at higher rather than low levels of assessment, and that there is little evidence that disaffection from the processes of education and attendant low achievement are specifically gender-related problems. They also demonstrate that gender differentials in achievement, where they do exist, are specific to certain subjects (Gorard *et al.* 1999). They identify English, languages, some design subjects and humanities as particular areas of female strength, with girls gaining more of the higher achievement levels:

> Otherwise the achievement gaps are static or declining. This provides an important corrective to many previous accounts of boys' 'underachievement'. Of course it remains a matter of concern that, in general terms, boys are performing less well than girls in many subjects, and also that any students of either gender appear to be underachieving.
>
> (Gorard *et al.* 1999: 450)

The ways in which the comparative achievement figures are arrived at have also been the subject of critical scrutiny. In their re-examination of the figures on assessment performance for Wales, Gorard *et al.* (1999) have argued that the gender performance analysis commonly cited is fundamentally flawed. There is, for example, a tendency to confuse percentages and percentage points, and a tendency not to use proportionate figures. In their consideration of the Welsh data for example, and taking into account comparable English data, Gorard *et al.* (1999: 452) conclude that these tell 'a compatible story of "stabilized disparity" between boys and girls, and smaller differences at lower grades' than other analyses would suggest.

There is little doubt that the actual evidence on gender and achievement gives a much more mixed picture of the relative performances of girls and boys than the 'moral panic' brigade would suggest. Moreover 'the blinkered preoccupation with achievement' (Mahony 1998: 44) masks much more complex relationships between gender and education. Over the past fifty years or so the educational performances of boys *and* girls have been on a rising trajectory. Boys and girls are both much more successful at school than they were ten, twenty or thirty years ago (Delamont 1999). Arnot *et al.* (1996, 1999), in research undertaken for the Equal Opportunities Commission, specifically addressed how English and Welsh education reforms of the late 1980s had impacted on gender equality (see also Salisbury 1996 for a summary of the Welsh data and Turner *et al.* 1995 for the comparable Scottish study). In their analysis of examination performance over a 10-year period (1985–94)

Arnot *et al*. (1996: xii) noted that 'trends in relation to gender at GCSE and A-level established before the reforms in terms of improving male and female entry and performance have continued throughout the period'. So any underperformance of boys needs to be seen in a relative rather than absolute context. The performance of girls and boys has been on an upward trajectory, and while there may be some evidence to suggest the trajectory for girls might be rising faster at some levels and in some subjects that does not necessarily culminate in any blanket underachievement for boys.

The claim to a wholesale phenomenon of the failure of boys may actually mask continuums of achievement and failure between boys and girls. For example, as Epstein *et al*. (1998: 11) argue, the 'overall underachievement of boys at school is a strongly classed and racialized phenomenon'. Sustained commentaries have singled out particular groups of young men as specifically failing categories – such as working-class boys and African-Caribbean boys. Chris Woodhead, Chief Inspector of Schools for England, reportedly said that the underachieving boy is one of the most disturbing problems facing the educational system, and he particularly singled out white working-class boys (see *Times Educational Supplement*, 19 March 1996; also Cohen 1998; Raphael Reed 1998). But there are challenges to this 'recent' discourse. Delamont (1999) reminds us that schools have failed to harness working-class boys to the academic curriculum for over a century. And Gorard *et al*. (1999) questioned whether disaffection and performance at the lower levels of the different scale is a gendered phenomenon at all.

Similar points have been made with regard to race. Sewell (1998) and others (see Mac an Ghaill 1988 and 1994; Gillborn 1995; Fordham 1996) have continued to question the homogeneity of experience attributed to black students:

> Not all black boys are the same. This may seem a simple or common-sense assertion but in terms of teacher perception and the popular discourses that underpin 'black masculinity' there is evidence of an acceptance of cultural and ethnic essentialism. [I] challenge the homogenisation of black (i.e. African-Caribbean) boys into one lump of rebellious, phallocentric underachievers.
>
> (Sewell 1998: 111)

Hence the claims to a wholesale phenomenon of male failure at school are at best only partially substantiated, and fail to make sense of the complexity of the relationships between boys and schooling. For example Mac an Ghaill (1996) among others has noted that sexuality and sexual politics are rarely explored in relation to gendered achievement (also see Epstein and Johnson 1998). Debates over failing boys also mask the realities that many boys continue to do extremely well at school (Power *et al*. 1998a). The reality is that the picture of gender and achievement is far from the simple equation that has recently been presented. Moreover 'full data on the intersection of "race", social class and gender in national patterns of achievement remains invaluable' (Raphael Reed 1998: 56).

In the light of this seeming complexity, and certainly inconclusiveness, it is perhaps surprising that the 'failing boys' story remains one of the central narratives in the discourse of contemporary education. A number of arguments have been articulated to *explain* the continuing 'belief' that boys are failing, and that schools are failing boys. These include articulations that masculinity is in crisis. In part this fits into contemporary scholarly and political interest in new men's and masculinity studies. Here the distinction has been made between pro-feminist work which 'actively engages with feminist theories, methodology and epistemologies as part of their research agendas' (Skelton 1998: 220) and work which aims to re-establish models of (white) heterosexual masculinities in the face of contemporary contradictions, crises and threats (not least from feminism). Jackson (1998) has argued that while the crisis of men and masculinities is not particularly new, there is mileage in the 'displacement consequences of boys' underachievement', framed in a context of standards and performance as the new rhetoric of schooling:

> The real power inequalities between boys and girls, and between dominant, white heterosexual boys and subordinated/complicated masculinities have been masked through this process of reframing. The old language of educational inequality has been replaced then by the language of boys' underachievement and male disadvantage.
>
> (Jackson 1998: 78)

While Jackson suggests that this 'feminist backlash' argument has merit, he is keen to establish that the subject of boys' underachievement is much more 'ambivalent and contradictory' than is suggested. Moreover, discourses of boys' underachievement can be constructive in redefining masculinities. The problem of underachieving boys can thus be viewed both as a strategy to reinstate hegemonic masculine discourses, and in part a feminist backlash. More constructively it could also be viewed as an, albeit inadequate, attempt at reconstructing and rethinking masculinities and identities:

> Feminism, Britain's decline as a major power in a post-colonial context, unemployment and so on have disrupted dominant, white, heterosexual masculinity as a taken for granted norm . . . and have begun to interrogate it. As conventional, heterosexual masculinity has become a more explicit and visible object of enquiry, a more nuanced, critical focus has emerged on the gendering, heterosexualizing and masculinizing of boys and men.
>
> (Jackson 1998: 80)

The feminization of teaching has also been held up as part of the 'problem of boys', although it is certainly not a new or wholly recent phenomenon that women make up the majority of the teaching labour force (Coffey and Delamont 2000). Feminism, and in particular women teachers, has been partially blamed for failing to provide an atmosphere suitable to foster success among boys. In an analysis of this argument, Delamont (1999: 14–15) lists a number of assumptions consistent with this position (reproduced below):

- It treats boys as an undifferentiated mass, all receiving the same treatment.
- It assumes all women teachers have signed up to 'progressive, anti-competitive nurturing vision of teaching, simultaneously rejected by all male teachers'.

- Male teachers are stereotyped as 'sports loving, fierce disciplinarians' auto-matically revered as male role models (and women teachers stereotyped as not providing appropriate role models for boys).
- It assumes that all female teachers are committed to feminism in theory *and* practice.
- It implies that women teachers value girls more than boys, and prefer to teach girls.
- It reveres a kind of 'golden age' when schools had lots of male staff, and no 'problems' of boys and underachievement existed.

Delamont asserts that none of these assumptions are actually supported by sustained empirical evidence. Furthermore, blaming the feminization of teaching for the underachievement of boys fails to conceptualize accurately either the results of the teachers' work, the teaching profession or the differentiated experience of boys (see Coffey and Delamont 2000). Indeed, even if teaching has been feminized in theory, policy and practice, *some* boys have done very well out of it!

There are a number of detrimental consequences of this preoccupation with the discourse of the underachieving boy as one of the dominant dis-courses of educational outcome. Buying into this discourse places us in danger of simplifying the relationships between gender, schooling and achievement, and in doing so masks the complexities of masculinities and femininities and how these interact with educational practice and outcomes. Thus it can serve actually to undermine and deny the success of girls and women in the educational system (and indeed the success of boys and young men). Examina-tion and other educational achievements are not celebrated. And feminism becomes something to blame, rather than a key player in the strides towards equality within education. Indeed, the failing boy discourse masks the reality that achievement for *both* sexes has been and is on a rising trajectory, while at the same time it encourages the reassertion of a discourse of hegemonic masculinity out of a seemingly straightforward debate about educational outcomes. As Raphael Reed (1999: 97) notes, 'a narrow focus on measurable outcomes inadequately captures the complexity of gender issues in education, and a broader concern with the "hidden curriculum" and social processes of schooling should remain a key priority'. However, the failing boys debate has been successful in raising the profile of gender and education to higher echelons than ever before. Gender (albeit boys) is now on policy agendas and increasing amounts of time, attention and resources are being directed to gender issues in school contexts. But, as Gorard *et al.* (1999) note, initiatives aimed at ameliorating the incidence of achievement gaps may be misplaced (as may be educational research in this area) without a more comprehensive and sensitive understanding of the actual patterns of differential attainment.

Educating for citizenship

One of the less tangible 'outcomes' of education enjoying a renewed political interest is the pursuit of 'active' citizenship. Citizenship is currently riding high on political and social policy agendas, in the UK and elsewhere (see Turner 1990; Bulmer and Rees 1996). In this young people have featured heavily (Jones and Wallace 1992; Morrow and Richards 1996). Where young people's transitions to adulthood have become increasingly theorized as problematic, citizenship has offered a useful framework for understanding the end product of youth and indeed schooling (Jones and Wallace 1992). Linked to this concern with citizenship has come a renewed emphasis on the role of education in fostering citizenship. This has led to exhortations to promote education for citizenship. The UK Commission on Citizenship (1990) recommended that citizenship should be part of each individual's education from early years, and that all educational programmes – compulsory, post-compulsory, non-compulsory, formal and informal – should incorporate considerations of citizenship. The UK government's Advisory Group on Education for Citizenship and the Teaching of Democracy in Schools has since recommended that citizenship education be a statutory part of pupils' educational entitlement, to be accompanied by specified learning outcomes (see Citizenship Advisory Group 1998). Citizenship education looks set to become part of the accepted discourse of the national curriculum and schooling.

It has been the notion of active citizenship that has informed this development of provision of citizenship education for young people. Beck (1996) finds it informs the curriculum guidance pertaining to education for citizenship in schools, and Evans (1995) identifies similar influences in the post-curricular and training field. Likewise it is active citizenship which informs projects such as the Millennium Volunteer and other volunteering schemes (see European Commission 1996). The notion of active citizenship (and the active citizen) combines communal values and social responsibilities with an ideological commitment to self-interest. Aimed as much as anything at disadvantaged youth (France 1996), active citizenship impresses on young people the responsibilities that come with the status of adult citizen. In this formulation 'active citizens are charitable, public spirited individuals who make a voluntary contribution to society at a local level' (Hall *et al.* 1998: 308). While the notion of active citizenship has substantially informed debates over education for citizenship, commentators have been quick to question the conceptualization of citizenship that is supported and proposed as an outcome of education (Hall *et al.* 1998). Harrison (1991) has stressed the differential nature of citizenship experiences. This is contrasted with observations that citizenship is, more often than not, conceptualized as a singular, undifferentiated and universal status (Hall *et al.* 1998), in contrast to the plural identities which young people are involved in negotiating as they navigate their way through education, and into adulthood. Hence in focusing on citizenship there is a danger of denying the lived realities of young people's experiences.

Attention has also focused on what education for citizenship actually means in practice. Beck (1996) for example found that provision for citizenship education in schools in Britain (albeit prior to the citizenship advisory group report and subsequent education developments) fell short of a commitment to open recognition and exploration of the complexity of the issues. It was premised on a particular version of active citizenship which young people were educated *for* rather than *about*. Similarly Evans (1995) found that vocational education and training initiatives of the 1980s and 1990s only embedded a minimal note of citizenship – predominantly instrumental and certainly not predicated on expansionist visions. Certainly there are concerns that an education for citizenship as currently proposed would ultimately serve to reflect an agenda that focuses on skills and competencies for active contribution to a fluid economy, as well as realigned understandings of nationalism and social responsibility. This is in marked contrast to more expansive, innovative and democratic understandings of citizenship espoused by, for example, the democratic schools movement (Gordon 1986; Smith *et al*. 1987, 1988; Harber and Meighan 1989).

Forms of citizenship education have always gone on in schools, but this is rarely discussed in the renewed calls for an increased role of education for citizenship in schools. Education has long been involved in teaching about the everyday experiences or realities of citizenship, and an outcome of the educational experience has long been the social reproduction of citizens. For example, commentators have systematically revealed the ways in which social class, race and gender are 'taught' as citizenship issues in schools (Gillborn 1992; Gordon 1992). Drawing on ethnographic fieldwork in England, for example, Gillborn argued that schools were already teaching about citizenship for black people in the UK. Drawing on an early curriculum guidance document (NCC 1990), Gillborn suggested that citizenship education discourse is in danger of ignoring 'the important day-to-day messages that schools transmit concerning the citizenship of their students, that is the degree to which students truly belong and may expect full participation and equal access within society' (Gillborn 1992: 59). Citizenship education is a worthy *outcome* aim of schooling, although there are degrees of contestation over its meaning and how it is delivered. Like the concept of citizenship itself there are different interpretations that can be levelled at education for citizenship, which reflect different agendas and different outcomes. Like other educational debates, the citizenship issue, and its operationalization in the school context, is in danger of oversimplifying the complexity of the reality – homogenizing the real heterogeneous experience of citizenship and social identity. Citizenship is at the heart of exploring the relationships between education, economy and society, and has at least two guises; 'on the one hand citizenship appears as a system of regulation and social control . . . on the other hand citizenship appears as a claim of rights, as a demand by the excluded for access and participation' (Connell 1992: 133). The contrast between the social control and social justice aspects of citizenship is a long-standing dichotomy within education. Debates over the place of citizenship in education systems will continue to remain as key markers of the contemporary relationships between education, economy, society and the state.

Conclusion

This chapter has sought to explore the relationships between education, economy and society through an exploration of educational outcomes. The focus of the chapter has been to map shifting understandings and visions of the aims of education, as they relate to issues of equality and difference. Underpinning the chapter is the dilemma of whether schooling (and education more generally) exists to reproduce or interrupt culture. A starting point was the (re)positioning of education in shifting economic and social times, and the consequences of this for the ways in which we chart and articulate educational outcomes and differences. This enables a recasting of educational outcome and achievement in terms of categories such as class, race and gender. The second half of the chapter considered two contemporary educational discourses – the phenomenon of the 'underachieving boy' and education for citizenship. The first enables a reformulating of debates about gender (race, class, sexuality) and achievement. The second leads to a much broader conceptualization of educational outcome, and strengthens the claim to a relationship between education and society in changing times. The next chapter shifts the focus from learners, and the educational outcomes in which they are immersed and assessed, to teachers. Teachers and teaching are central to the process and outcomes of education. They are at the 'chalk face' of classroom contexts and are also the frontline implementers of educational policy. Both the everyday work of teaching, and the teaching profession, have been challenged, changed and recast during the latter part of the twentieth century.

7 Teachers *and* teaching

Introduction

Teachers are central to the day-to-day work of the school, and serve as key implementers of educational policy. As primary social actors in education, teachers are engaged in the everyday accomplishment of pedagogic practice as well as the transmission of knowledge and skills. They are also responsible for the everyday management of classrooms. Moreover, teachers are at the front line or the 'chalk face' of educational policy and change. Hence teachers and teaching are critical to contemporary understandings of education and schooling. Teachers have been a familiar and recurrent subject of educational and sociological research, although research emphases have changed over time. This reflects trends in research disciplines, as well as the shifting nature of the work of teaching. Biddle *et al.* (1997) document the different perspectives that have emerged in the literature – and distinguish between classic and alternative visions of teaching research. The two classic 'research' views they describe are concerned with, first, the official capacities of teachers and second, the realities of the classroom. The former emphasizes the official capacity of teachers as (state) employees, with agreed rights and responsibilities. This perspective of the teacher tends to ignore both the moral character of education and the interactive process of schooling, and is often foreshadowed in debates over the failure of schools, and political rhetoric encapsulated in the discourse of derision (Ball 1990). In other words, the failure of teachers to 'do their job properly' has been blamed for the (perceived poor) state of education.

The second classic research position highlighted by Biddle *et al.* (1997) locates teachers within their professional role in the school and classroom setting. This perspective tends to focus on 'dilemmas that are created for teachers by limited budgets, unbending curricula, public disputes about education, diffuse goals for schools, unruly students, and the fact that teachers normally have low status in the bureaucratic organisation of the school system' (Biddle *et al.* 1997: 2). Intermittently, these classical research perspectives have been joined by alternative visions and approaches. These have taken a number of different forms and have reflected changes both in the work of teachers and in the research discourses that aim to describe that work.

These different perspectives have included (among others) neo-Marxist, feminist and racialized accounts, all of which have focused on the agency of teachers in the processes of social (re)production that permeate school and classroom life. They have variously been concerned with mapping the (changing) demographic characteristics of teachers and with fieldwork that attempts to chart and make sense of teacher behaviour and the interactional qualities of teaching. There has also been a recent focus on the careers, lives and identities of teachers, and the ways in which the teacher self is constructed and (re)produced (see Chapter 5, this volume). In addition, changes to educational policy and practice have often acted as catalysts to studies of teacher reform and professional responses to educational change.

Sociological research on education has contributed a significant corpus of material on the lives and work of teachers. This material has drawn on a diverse set of perspectives, and contributed to a variety of understandings of teachers – as professionals, workers and vehicles of the state, as well as individuals involved in the construction and (re)production of their own identities and the identities of others. This chapter takes as a focus the lives and work of teachers, set against a backdrop of educational change. The experiences of teachers and the shifts (and continuities) in their everyday work and professional lives ultimately can reveal much about particular aspects of contemporary education. Considering teachers and teaching enables the exploration and documentation of the relationship between the state and a significant group of professions, and the saliency of identity work in a time of substantial policy and social change.

This chapter is organized into four main sections. First, the changing world and work of the teacher is briefly mapped out, enabling the relationships between policy, practice and everyday realities to be explored. Second, the training of teachers is explored as an example of the shifting relationships between state, educational policy and practice. The changes that have occurred in the teacher education programmes and ethos are significant. They ultimately affect the ways in which education is perceived and delivered. The third section considers the changes and continuities in the everyday work of classroom teachers. This reveals the multiplicity of roles and responsibilities that are present in the negotiation of relationships between teachers and learners, in the context of educational institutions. Lastly, the cultural–political context of contemporary teaching is briefly considered. Teaching cannot be separated from wider issues of equality and social justice, or from its social contexts. Thus this section explores these relationships through the exploration of some contemporary case studies.

The changing world of teachers

The way in which education is organized has undergone significant change over recent decades, as this volume has documented. To a large extent this reflects broader changes in contemporary, advanced industrial societies. The establishment of quasi-markets and the moves toward devolved state education have ironically been coupled with increased control over curricula and the work of teachers. These 'new times' (Whitty 1997: 300) of educational policy and practice emphasize choice and diversity. However, their consequences have not been all positive. One response to these policy changes has been to highlight the ways in which this increased emphasis on diversity and difference celebrates the multiple and fractured identities of a postmodern society. Others, however, have noted the intensification of social difference that has resulted (Kenway 1993; Gewirtz *et al.* 1995), and the changes and additional pressures that have been placed on the teaching profession as front-line implementers of educational change. Teachers, and the work that they do, have been heavily implicated in these new educational trends. Thus, the teaching profession is in the process of being reformed, and teacher subjectivities reconstituted. As Whitty (1997: 304–5) has noted, 'those changes that are taking place in the nature of educational governance and in management practices in schools clearly impact upon the character of teachers' professional lives'. There are a number of specific, though interrelated, ways in which the everyday world and work of the teacher has been affected by the broader policy changes.

Recruitment and training

Teacher training and recruitment were the subject of substantial debate and policy reform during the 1980s and 1990s. This topic is discussed in detail in the next substantive section of this chapter. To summarize here, new structures have been established to manage teacher training in England and Wales. Alongside these have come renewed concerns about the standard of teacher recruitment and enhanced strategies to improve recruitment levels. Shifts in educational policy, and concerns over educational practice, have focused attention on the training regimes of new teachers, and the knowledge and pedagogical shifts they are presented with. This has had consequences for new recruits to teaching, teacher educators and institutions of higher education, as well as teacher-mentors and practice schools.

Changing organization of schools

Schools themselves have also undergone fundamental reorganization as a result of educational policy reform. Local management of schools, the move to grant maintained status for some, and the implementation of a quasi-market in state education have impacted on the work of all teachers (and not just those in positions of management). Teachers spend increasing amounts of their time involved in the business of marketing the school, and undertaking administration. There are contested claims that initiatives, such as local management, have increased the decision-making potential of teachers. There is little doubt that changes have brought about increased administrative, managerial and resourcing responsibilities.

Curriculum changes

The introduction of national curricula in England and Wales (and the introduction of similar structures elsewhere, for example Northern Ireland and

Scotland), and the new assessment structures which underpin them, have had profound impacts on the everyday work of the classroom teacher, as well as establishing new regimes for schools more generally. The establishment of a national curriculum has dictated not only what is to be taught (hence reducing teachers' autonomy over their curriculum content, to the extent that they ever had any) but also the pedagogical strategies for transmission *and* the criteria by which assessment standards are judged. This has direct effects on the potential for teacher agency in the classroom and the nature of professional autonomy. The implementation of the curriculum has also increased the workloads of the classroom teacher, through the preparation of new materials and execution of new assessment regimes.

Accountability and effectiveness

A result of the wider educational and school-based changes has been the degree to which teachers have become subjected to increased scrutiny. As Whitty (1997: 303) has argued,

> There has been something of a move away from the notion that the teaching profession should have a professional mandate to act on behalf of the state in the best interests of its citizens, to a view that teachers (and indeed, other professions) need to be subjected to the rigours of the market and/or greater control and surveillance, on the part of the re-formed state.

There have been a series of attempts to increase control, surveillance and supervision of teachers, at both individual and professional levels. This has included enhanced control over what is taught and how, the re-forming of teacher education, proposed introductions for performance-related pay, and a series of measures designed to reward good teachers and ostracize (or indeed remove) 'bad' ones. In establishing these new rhetorics of accountability and effectiveness, educational reforms have played a part in responding to a discourse of decision, which has systematically attacked the teaching profession, and implicated poor teachers and teaching in concerns over educational standards.

These are just some of the ways in which the teacher's life and work has shifted as a result of educational reform. Changes have occurred at the level of the teaching profession and in higher echelons of school management. The day-to-day work of the classroom teacher has also changed. The relationships between the teacher, the teaching profession, the school and the state have been and are still in the process of being reformed. However, we should not overestimate these changes. Despite substantial change, much continuity remains.

- Teachers are still the front-line providers of education; classrooms still need to be managed and organized, lessons planned, students engaged, encouraged, taught and controlled.
- Teaching remains concerned with social process and social interaction. The articulation of relationships between teachers and learners is still central to the process, function and 'success' of education systems.

- Teachers still have careers, lives and histories that are situated within the work they do and the experiences they have. These identities are (still) mediated by cultural politics, class, race, gender, and sexuality.

A consideration of the life and work of the contemporary teacher must navigate between the recognition of change and the robustness of continuity. The world of the teacher has changed, and will probably continue to do so in the light of further policy implementation. At the same time the everyday realities of classroom work have considerable similiarity with the past (and most likely future) world of teaching. As was outlined earlier, one area of significant change has been that of teacher education and training. This has had profound impacts on teacher educators and institutions of higher education, as well as (new) teachers and schools. It is to this area that the chapter now turns.

(Re)training the teachers

Teacher education in the UK has undergone dramatic changes in the past few decades (Furlong *et al.* 1988, 1996; Edwards 1990; Gosden 1990; Maguire 1995; Mahony 1997). Policies have set about reforming the practice and ethos of teacher education. Moreover, as Mahony (1997) argues, these reforms have international comparability and reflect local (national) educational climates, as well as more general international changes in the public sector. In practical terms these changes have meant a number of things. University departments, responsible for initial teacher education, have been closed, merged and reconstituted. Alternative routes into teaching (for example licensed and articled teachers, see Furlong *et al.* 1996) have been approved. Tighter teaching standards have been developed and introduced (not least through the setting up of the Teaching Training Agency). There has been a tightening of control over what is taught to teachers in training in terms of knowledge and pedagogy. Changes have affected the structure, organization, curriculum and ethos of teacher recruitment and training. Teacher education has been vulnerable to shifting demographic and economic contexts, and to political fluctuations in educational policy. Like teaching more generally, teacher education has been recast within a discourse of educational effectiveness (Mahony and Hexhall 1997). In England and Wales emphasis has increasingly been placed on the practical, competence-based skills of teaching, and the consequent restructuring of teacher education to ensure that these are prioritized in training programmes.

> In the UK the teacher is being reconstructed as the practical person, the doer not the thinker, the manager not the scholar. This new teacher will be cheaper to produce because what is required is more practical experience and less theoretical interrogation of schooling and pedagogy.
>
> (Maguire 1995: 119)

The sustained attack on teacher education, primarily by the New Right, has been consolidated by what Mahony (1997) calls 'The New Public Management' (NPM) approach in teacher education. This has promoted the view that the initial education of teachers should be primarily concerned with attributes and skills for classroom practice, narrowly defined, assuming that the skills and attributes deemed necessary for teaching can readily be standardized and controlled, monitored and checked. At the same time this approach marginalizes theoretical concerns and the contribution of academic disciplines to teaching and teacher education. In England and Wales, for example, the establishment of CATE (the Council for the Accreditation of Teacher Education) in 1984 began this trend toward standardization and overt assessment. CATE assessed already existing initial teacher education programmes, using criteria that pertained to a number of parameters such as selection procedures, teacher educators and curriculum content. CATE was superseded by the Teacher Training Agency (TTA) in 1994. The shift in teacher education content has been more dramatic since, with an increasing concentration on the teacher's operational and utilitarian role within the classroom, and the continual downplaying of theoretical perspectives and social contexts.

The virtual removal of theoretical perspectives from teacher education (Acker 1994, for example, has noted the virtual disappearance of sociology from the curriculum of teacher education) has been combined with an increasingly centralized teacher training curriculum. New models of teacher education are more befitting of a workplace-training model, with an emphasis upon training-on-the-job and studying in school (Furlong *et al.* 1996; Hodkinson and Hodkinson 1999). In this sense, teaching is being reconceptualized as a job requiring common sense, practical experience and training, rather than necessarily a (post)graduate, higher education. With this has come an increasing emphasis on partnership between higher education institutions and schools (Goodlad 1991; Edwards 1995). Similar trends have been noted elsewhere, for example in the USA (Bullough 1997) and Australia (Nance and Fawns 1993).

These changes have been criticized on a number of different levels. They challenge and disrupt teacher autonomy, and the professional status of teachers. They have a direct impact on how the work of teaching is conceptualized, understood and reproduced. The changes to teacher education have also been attacked for their lack of attention to issues of social justice and equal opportunities. For example, feminist scholars and others have noted that the reforms to teacher education have done little to prioritize equality and social justice (Mahony 1997; Coffey and Delamont 2000). An increased emphasis on the standards of teaching might well have had centralized issues of equal opportunity, gender equality and other issues of social justice (such as race). Yet the reforms have impeded rather than aided attempts at integrating theory and practice, and have perhaps generated more apathy than action to social justice concerns. CATE, in the UK, never prioritized gender, choosing to refer to it only under more general guises of equal opportunities, personal and social education and so forth – to be permeated rather than prioritized in the teaching curriculum. While CATE increased its reference to gender over the years, taking advice from the Equal Opportunities Commission (see for example EOC 1989), its overall commitment remained rather low. While there has been lip service to a commitment to gender equality (as part of a more general commitment to equality), teacher education has failed to provide the opportunity for theoretical reflections on gender regimes. Gender still holds this rather tenuous and marginal position in a full and time-constrained teacher training curriculum (Coffey 1992; Acker 1994; Coffey and Delamont 2000).

The Teacher Training Agency for England was tasked with moving the reforms of teacher education forward. Two of the appointed members of the TTA board were drawn from right-wing educational pressure groups, responsible for the earlier sustained attacks on the theoretical (anti-racist, anti-sexist, feminist) elements of teacher education (see Ball 1990). The TTA remit and consequent restructuring of teacher education made no mention of the needs of teachers to be educated in matters relating to social justice, such as gender (Mahony and Hexhall 1997). Raising the standards of teacher education and training did not, it would appear, include an appreciation of the political, social and cultural contexts of schooling, education and teaching:

> Teaching involves relationships between people whose personal, social, economic, cultural and political identities and positionings are complex. Negotiating and succeeding within this arena calls for sophisticated everyday repertoires of skills which teachers constantly need to develop. Reference to such creative professionalism is, however, absent from the TTA's documentation which instead concentrates almost entirely on concerns about teachers' subject knowledge and pupil performance, both of which are treated as desituated.
>
> (Mahony and Hexhall 1997: 143)

As Mahony and Hexhall (1997) note, the only area in which the TTA specifically acknowledged issues of gender was recruitment. Here priority was given to recruiting more men into teaching (TTA 1996). One implication of this is that the feminization of teaching is seen as part of the 'problem' of the teaching profession. This is not unrelated to the moral panic over the teaching and education of boys (see Chapter 6 for a detailed discussion). Mahony's (1997) analysis of the new public management ethos illuminates the ways in which the heavy emphasis on standards, output and effectiveness has served to marginalize the social justice contexts of teaching and learning. In the reconstituted teacher education there is little (no) emphasis on the social and political contents of teaching generally. Rendered mute are a wide range of issues that could, and arguably *should*, be at the very heart of debates about educational outcomes and standards, for example the gendered and racialized contexts of schooling, relations between teachers and pupils and the socio-economic and class-based inequalities in educational opportunities and outcomes.

Teacher educators are referred to by Maguire (1995) as the 'hidden teachers', central to the reconstitution and reorganization of initial teacher training. As reforms increasingly centre this training in schools, teacher educators within higher education become increasingly vulnerable, as staffing strategies shift. Goodlad (1991) argued that, increasingly, education faculty have distanced themselves from teacher education and the careers of teachers. This is perhaps not surprising given that the policies that govern teacher education are now set outside higher education (although it remains a mute point whether it was ever thus). Teacher educators have very little autonomy over the curricular and academic development of teacher education and training. In the UK this has arguably meant a diminishing of the role of higher education in the training of the classroom teacher. Whitehead *et al.* (1996) note that as student teachers spend less time in higher education institutions, teacher educators face reductions in their staffing base. They report the non-replacement of staff, the use of temporary appointments, earlier retirement packages and the employment of 'visiting' lecturers paid on an hourly basis, as evidence of a move to an increasingly casualized and transient teacher education workforce. While policy rhetoric may rephrase this in terms of flexibility, the outcome is much the same. As an area of higher education which has conventionally seen more women employed than in other fields, changes to teacher education also have gendered consequences. Indeed, one of the conventional areas of female employment in HE is in the process of contracting and reconstituting (Coffey and Delamont 2000). Ironically, the resultant higher education labour market opportunities – 'flexible' (temporary) contracts, or 'visiting' rather than permanent status – may actually increase the feminization process of the teacher education workforce. It is well documented that women are more likely to be found in such 'transient' and insecure employment. Whitty (1997: 345) has made a similar point about changes to the context of teaching more generally, arguing that factors such as the 'substitution of full-time, permanent, qualified, and experienced staff by part-time, temporary, less qualified and less experienced' alternatives leaves women teachers particularly vulnerable to exploitation.

These trends in teacher education can be seen within a framework of higher education. Teacher education institutions, and education departments in the university sector in the UK, have been pushed to adapt and survive. Alongside the shifts in initial (and in-service) teacher education provision, there has been a series of general changes. These have meant (among other things) a requirement that departments seek additional sources of funding (for example by recruiting overseas students onto advanced courses) and maintain (and develop in some instances) a robust publishing and research grant base. This has further increased workloads and pressures on staff who have also been hit by the same destabilizing forces affecting all of higher education, making long-term planning of staffing and courses problematic. Inside the university sector (certainly in the UK) few rewards are forthcoming to those involved in the training and education of occupational groups such as teachers, nurses or social workers. An increasingly dominant emphasis on research funding and output makes it increasingly unattractive (and non-viable) to be a department or individual mainly concerned with teaching and learning. This is compounded by the ever more stringent quality requirements within higher education – teaching quality assessments, internal and external audits and reviews, lengthy documentation, recognizable and measurable aims and objectives and so forth. These parallel the teaching quality requirements within schools (see Chapter 2). In all, 'schools of education have had to face *both* the incursions into academic freedom and security suffered by higher education *and* the fall out from the government's educational reforms in the schools and alterations of teacher education' (Acker 1994: 18, her emphasis).

Maguire (1995) has argued that there is still a commitment to a theoretical base in teacher education among teacher educators. But in their everyday reality, teacher educators are faced with a new dominant discourse of the 'practical', which both idealizes and misrepresents practice, and limits learning to the reproduction of the immediate and routine. Maguire points to factors such as the perceived need for immediacy, the time constraints of initial teacher training programmes, and the 'survival' skills approach to early teaching experiences as compounding the difficulties that teacher educators have in reconciling theory and practice. In attempting to meet the longer term professional needs of student teachers, while helping them 'survive' the first year(s) of school, it is more often than not the matters of reflection, interpersonal relationships, values and theoretically informed 'professional' knowledge that will fall by the wayside. This, of course, means a privileging of the technical on-the-job skills of the classroom and subject specialist knowledge. This in turn presents enormous difficulties for putting and keeping on the agenda broader issues such as social justice, interpersonal skills and reflexivity.

The contemporary conditions of work for teacher educators bear remarkable similarities to the everyday realities of school classroom teachers. The new and ever increasing pressures of the reforms to teacher education have meant that survival becomes a dominant goal, displacing innovation and reflection. The publication of national standards (TTA 1998) is further evidence that teacher education is undergoing a reconceptualization – away from notions of reflection and towards measurable effectiveness. Initial teacher education courses have always been criticized for being too short to include all that is desirable as well as all that is required (Coffey and Acker 1991). Survival thus is not only prioritized on teacher education courses, but is also a lived reality for teacher educators. Given current pressures on teachers and teacher educators, and an increasingly prescriptive curriculum and pedagogic strategy, it is unsurprising that simple, non-controversial and survival-based teaching styles are adopted (Shah 1989). What this means is that new teachers are being equipped with the tools for survival (perhaps), but not necessarily the theoretical and pedagogic resources to develop innovative, critical social justice perspectives on classroom practice. This has fundamental ramifications for the future of teaching and learning in schools, and presents a one-dimensional and, more importantly, an unrealistic portrayal of the complexities of everyday classroom life. The next section of this chapter explores this aspect of teaching, by focusing on the day-to-day work of the teacher.

The everyday work of the classroom teacher

The largest part of the everyday work of the majority of teachers takes place 'at the chalk face' in the classroom. Of course, teachers also play roles in the wider school and community; managing out-of-school activities; taking part in meetings and administration; engaging in promotional and marketing activities; community and parental liaison. Indeed, many of these activities have undergone significant changes with recent educational reforms. Issues of school choice and parental preference have, for example, exaggerated the importance of relationships between parents, schools and teachers (David 1993; Vincent 1996). Teachers have increasingly been expected to undertake the tasks of school management, and partake in the discourse of accountability. This is in addition to their teaching tasks (Whitty 1997). Teachers have also been required to devote more of their time to promotional and marketing activities (Cave and Wilkinson 1990; Gray 1992; Hesketh and Knight 1998; Maguire *et al.* 1999). This wider school and policy regime has permeated the classroom and the routine work of teachers. At the same time teachers have continued to undertake primary responsibility for managing the classroom and the learning process. Teachers are still tasked with the control, organization, transmission and reproduction of knowledge in the educational environment. As chapters in this volume have shown, recent educational reforms have had a significant impact on these tasks.

However, with change has also come continuity. Jackson's *Life in Classrooms* (1968) highlighted that classroom teachers must operate under conditions which require a sense of immediacy and 'front-stage' work (Goffman 1959). The front of the classroom remains the teacher's stage (Tartwijk *et al.* 1998). Much of the teacher's work requires immediate decisions about immediate situations. Stone (1993) uses the postmodern term 'contingency' to characterize this phenomenon. Fenwick's (1998) characterization of the teacher's work as the management of energy is one way in which this immediacy or contingency is enacted. Drawing on Koerner's (1992) description of the 'body electric' classroom, Fenwick (1998: 624–5) argues that

> A group of adolescents in a classroom appear at times to be a bubbly cauldron of physical energy . . . the fidgety restlessness and raw, unpredictable spurts of mood and behaviour that wriggle in complex dynamics underneath the tidy classroom structures. Teachers must interact with this energy within the relatively small confines of the classroom.

As Fenwick suggests, part of the teacher's daily task remains the direction of this energy of the classroom, often responding to immediate and unpredictable situations. Thus the need for immediacy is accompanied by individual teacher autonomy. The layout of the school, with classrooms often physically isolated from one another, means that professional colleagues are often out of reach of each other as they undertake their daily classroom work. How teachers respond to immediate situations – what goes on behind the classroom door – is for the realm of each individual teacher, albeit within professional and institutional parameters. The world of the classroom can thus be a very private world. This apparent autonomous (and relatively powerful) position of the classroom teacher has come under threat in recent years, as educational policy has increasingly dictated what should be taught and how teachers should go about that task (Apple 1986; Acker 1989, 1994; Ball 1990; Gray *et al.* 1999). For example, the introduction of a national curriculum in England and Wales, and a rigorous school (and teaching) inspection system (Apple 1998; Gray *et al.* 1999) has served to challenge the position of the classroom teacher as autonomous professional. The twin requirements of responding to immediate situations and an increasingly centralized controlling of classroom work make it increasingly difficult to introduce innovation into the classroom. As Acker (1994) and others have noted, school-based classroom initiatives (such as gender or race initiatives) are relatively unsuccessful – as teachers are increasingly time pressured, as well as working in the relatively private world of the classroom. One way in which teachers manage classroom space is through the establishment of routines and planned arrangements (Fenwick 1998). The management of the unpredictability of student energy relies to a large extent on the predictability of the teacher. Any additional initiatives, however deserving, create extra burdens on individual teachers, which are often too much to bear.

Commentators have increasingly recognized the pressures classroom teachers must now work under (Easthope and Easthope 2000). Increased centralized control of some aspects of the teacher's work (for example control over the curriculum and preferred pedagogical style) has been matched by decentralization of other aspects (for example, through the local management of schools). Both have changed the everyday regimes in which teachers routinely work. However, it is important to balance these 'cries of despair'. Local management of schools may offer some opportunities for autonomy in schools and classrooms, albeit restrictedly so. Equally the classroom teacher still retains relative autonomy over the organization and control of the classroom, and the effective delivery of the curriculum (albeit one which is imposed rather than self-defined). Teachers still undertake the primary responsibility for the determination of routines, rules and sanctions in the classroom (Coloroso 1982; Denscombe 1985; McLaughlin 1991; Gregg 1995). Classroom management is still a central part of the everyday work of the teacher:

> Teachers determine rules and routines which, in the classroom of an experienced teacher, function almost invisibly to display teacher expectations for behaviour, and to control student movement and distribution of materials. Teachers also intentionally create physical structures (i.e. arranging desks, sequencing activity, keeping a blackboard list of 'problem students') that encourage or repress certain behaviours.
>
> (Fenwick 1998: 621)

The classroom teacher still largely defines what acceptable behaviour is and what appropriate sanctions should be taken in the case of unacceptable behaviour. Woods (1990) notes that the role of the teacher remains a conflictual one. Colleagues often judge teachers on their ability to exercise discipline in their classrooms (McPherson 1972; Gregg 1995). Effective classroom management is about creating the right balance: between work and play; quiet and talk; student responsibility and external control, as well as ensuring that the classroom space is a 'safe place' (Fenwick 1998). Research has consistently demonstrated that teachers tend to concentrate on certain kinds of disruptive behaviour in the classroom. Paechter (1998), for example, suggests that they focus on disruption to the overt instructional context of the learning environment. As a consequence, overt and noisy styles of disaffection and disruption (primarily found among boys) are given more teacher attention. Some have argued that male disruptive behaviour in the classroom – boisterousness, competitiveness – may even be praised (Connell *et al.* 1982; Kessler *et al.* 1985). In comparison, teachers often see girls as passive, controllable and submissive, and there follows an expectation of good behaviour (Robinson 1992). Similar arguments have focused on the racialized contexts of control, highlighting the (white) teacher responses to different kinds of resistance behaviour (Mac an Ghaill 1988; Gillborn 1990; Troyna 1993a). These kinds of observations feed into the issue of control within the classroom. A common assumption is that a competent teacher is one who can keep a class quiet; for a quiet class is one that can be managed, and effective learning achieved (Robinson 1992). A number of studies have argued that the culture and ethos of school discipline often revolves around certain kinds of masculine behaviour (see Beynon 1989; Connell 1987; Shakeshaft 1989; Davies 1992). As Robinson (1992) notes, male teachers are more able to use overt forms of discipline and physical force in controlling a class. Davies (1992: 128) argues that the version of masculinity which has come to dominate school management is 'competitive, point scoring, over confident, sporting, career and status conscious' – with pupils clearly identifying discipline with physical intimidation and aggression (see also Askew and Ross 1988; Bailey 1996). Studies have demonstrated the ways in which discipline in schools is gendered (Cunnison 1989; Bailey 1996; Haywood and Mac an Ghaill 1996) and the consequences this has for seeking out alternative approaches based on cooperation and democratic principles (Harber and Meighan 1989).

Another focus of research on the everyday contexts of classroom teaching has been the ways in which teachers manage talk and interaction as part of their daily work. Classrooms are inherently interactive (verbal) environments, and the teacher's task remains one of participating in, and controlling, talk. Much of what the teacher actually does involves talking to pupils – individually and collectively, and creating a learning environment by balancing quiet and talk (Fenwick 1998). Early sociological work on the discourse and language of education highlighted the ways in which the 'words' of education have consequences in terms of social class (Bernstein 1971). More recently attention has turned to the racialized, gendered and sexualized contexts and consequences of educational discourses (Troyna 1993a; Weiner 1994; Fordham 1996; Epstein and Johnson 1998; Paechter 1998). There have been shifts in research emphasis. For example, work on gender and interaction has examined sexist terminology in everyday language (see Spender 1985; Ehrlich and King 1992) and the nature (and difference) of male and female discourse (Coates and Cameron 1989; Graddol and Swann 1989). It is now increasingly focused on recognizing the multiplicity of classroom voices, and how they are positioned as dominant or deficit; conceptualized as the norm or other (Paechter 1998). Hence the generalizations which have been repeatedly substantiated about (gender) imbalance in teacher attention (French and French 1993; Swann and Graddol 1994) and the different types of interaction engaged in with boys and girls (Sadker and Sadker 1985; Evans 1988) are still relevant to understanding classroom life. But, at the same time, more complex understandings of the relationships between educational settings and 'voice' have emerged. This has contributed to two realizations: that classroom talk is central to the learning and teaching process, and that 'in schools there is a wide range of voices, reflecting differences not just of gender but of "race", social class and "ability". Some are powerful and easily heard, some are positioned as Other' (Paechter 1998: 80).

This section has concentrated on some of the everyday aspects of the teacher's work, and considered these in terms of changes, continuities and shifting research and policy discourses. There is little doubt that the world of the classroom teacher has undergone substantial change in recent times. Teachers' time and space have been redefined, and have ironically become both more privatized *and* more public. At the same time, it is important to recognize and remember the enduring qualities and experiences of the front line of classroom teaching. In the next section of this chapter these classroom experiences are further explored through a brief consideration of the cultural politics of teaching.

Teaching in (post)modern times

Teachers are social actors operating in social and cultural contexts. They work within social institutions, and are also part of a wider society. They are routinely engaged in the negotiating of their own identity, and the shaping of the identities of others. In Chapter 5, the shaping of student and teacher identities and biographies were explored in some detail. Here, the wider dimensions of the teacher's work and world are briefly considered, focusing on the ways in which teaching is enmeshed within, and is undertaken through, a framework of cultural politics. Issues such as gender, sexuality and race *both* structure the everyday realities of the teacher *and* situate the work of teaching. Teaching takes place in gendered, racialized and sexualized settings, and hence serves as an important interface between young people and the wider socio-cultural world of which they are part. To illustrate this, three contemporary teaching 'debates' are considered here. These debates connect policy, research and teaching within a framework of cultural politics of difference.

The feminization of teaching thesis

The feminization thesis has at least two interpretations – that of numbers and that of ethos. While it is possible to argue with some degree of confidence that the first kind of feminization is visible (the international teaching force is majority female), the second kind of feminization – suggesting new structures, organization and ways of seeing and working – is much harder to substantiate. While the majority of teachers are women, the position of men and women in the teaching profession as a whole mirrors their position within international labour markets; the numbers of women securing senior teaching posts remain disproportionately low (Bell and Chase 1993; Acker

1994; Taylor 1995; Boulton and Coldron 1998; DfEE 1998a). While it is the case that women are educating the majority of children in the school classroom, women do not have systematic access to power and policy within the education system (Chase 1995; Turner *et al.* 1995). Nor have they been able to substantially influence the knowledge base of teaching and teacher education (Coffey 1992; Mahony 1997). Thus, while teaching has become increasingly *feminized* in terms of numbers, it has not become distinctly *feminist* in terms of career trajectories, discourse and ethos. This is not to say that there are not feminist teachers, feminist knowledge or feminist pedagogies at work in school classrooms (see Coffey and Delamont 2000). But the impact of these in terms of whole schools or education systems has been, and look set to continue to be, limited.

Teaching careers have gendered trajectories and gender has not been systematically addressed in teacher education. Neither of these have prevented the feminization thesis and attendant debate from contributing to concerns over educational standards and the gender climate of schooling. In this sense, the feminization of teaching (whether or not it is real, or how it is calculated) has been increasingly seen as 'part of the problem' of the profession – responsible for the perceived lack of discipline and control within schools; the introduction of 'soft' teaching styles and pedagogic strategies; falling educational standards; and the corruption of school knowledge. The feminization thesis has also been cited as a contributing factor in the moral panic over teaching and the education of boys. The Teacher Training Agency, set up to reform and monitor teacher education in England and Wales, only acknowledges issues of gender, with respect to recruitment. A priority has been given to the recruitment of more men into teaching (TTA 1996; Mahony and Hexhall 1997). Debates over the perceived underachievement of boys and the relationships between masculinities and schooling have an educational 'policy' impact of placing increased emphasis on the need to recruit more positive male role models into the teaching profession (Connell 1995; Haywood and Mac an Ghaill 1996).

The thesis of feminization situates teaching within a field of cultural and gender politics. It does so in a number of ways.

- The distinction between who teaches *and* the politics and process of teaching is recognized.
- The profile of teaching as a gendered (racialized, sexualized, fragmented) profession and work is revealed.
- The situated contexts of pedagogy and knowledge are substantiated – there are a variety of knowledges and pedagogies potentially open to teachers – and therefore those that are 'legitimated' and 'assumed' are necessarily partial.
- Teachers and teaching are part of the educational and school environment in which identities (masculinities, femininities) are negotiated and constructed.
- Commentators have identified relationships between the socio-cultural (gendered) construction of the teaching profession *and* educational outcomes. This can include examination performance, but also relates to civic and personal education.

Teachers and the (re)production of racism

During the 1990s, a methodological debate ensued within the sociology of education. This methodological dialogue broadly had two sides. On one side stood commentators such as Foster, Gomm and Hammersley (Foster 1992, 1993; Hammersley 1995; Foster *et al.* 1996; Foster and Hammersley 1998). On the other were David Gillborn and his colleagues working in the field of race and education (Gillborn and Drew 1993; Troyna 1993a; Gillborn 1995, 1998). The debate essentially revolved around issues of politics and equity (as well as methodology – see Chapter 8). More specifically, Foster and his colleagues systematically criticized educational researchers who, they argued, have participated in a project of deception in order to convince readers of racialized educational inequalities (that in fact do not exist). The debate has revolved around the presence or absence of racial injustice in educational settings. A number of influential studies have explored, through ethnographic and complementary quantitative data, the racialized contexts and experiences of schooling. In these studies, authors have highlighted the ways in which educational opportunities and school interactions are mediated by race and racism (see Mac an Ghaill 1988; Gillborn 1990; Wright 1992; Gillborn and Gipps 1996). While studies such as these have accumulated substantial data on the intended and unintended consequences of schooling and teacher behaviour on the racialized experiences of schooling, Foster and his colleagues have taken issue with their claims. They have done so on a number of levels: that the data are unconvincing; that the research is politically motivated and that political motivation compromises the research endeavour; and, for our purposes here, that such research victimizes teachers.

The area of race and racism is, of course, open to considerable debate and interpretation. As Gillborn attests, scholarly research should be open to critical scrutiny. However, the critique by Foster *et al.* enshrines an understanding of racism based on the notion of intent and action. Hence what they address is the presence of discriminatory teacher action, while ignoring unintentional or institutional racism (see Gillborn 1995; also Foster 1993 for a defence of this position). According to Gillborn (1998), this position has established a framework for interpreting teacher–student interactions in particular ways, and does not enable critical reflections of the relationships between teachers and students, based on student perceptions and everyday realities. 'It reduces institutional racism to the status of mere theoretical possibility. It results in a position that effectively denies teacher racism any major role as an explanatory (or even descriptive) concept in relation to the lived experience of minority students' (Gillborn 1998: 63).

Foster *et al.* have concluded that there is little (if any) reason to believe that ethnic minority students are disadvantaged by the actions of teachers and other school processes. This is in stark contrast to a body of evidence that articulates the racialized discourses of teaching and the experience of students. Moreover, the critique which Foster and his colleagues have embarked upon sets out to defend teachers, suggesting that other studies which have 'revealed' the racist contexts of teaching have unfairly victimized teachers. Again Gillborn (1995) argues that this represents a woefully simplistic understanding of research on the relationships between schooling, teaching and racism:

> Most of the work Foster criticizes seeks to understand teachers' actions and perspectives as they are created and modified through multiple interactions in complex organisational settings. True much of this work is critical, but none amounts to blanket condemnation of teachers as a group. Teachers have led many antiracist initiatives and most writers assign them a crucial role in moving towards a more equitable education system.
>
> (Gillborn 1995: 56)

This particular exchange has raised a number of important issues about the pursuit of educational research (which are examined in more detail in Chapter 8). It locates the educational research project within a framework of politics, ethics and issues of social justice, and raises important issues about the interpretation of data and the definitions that are employed. For the purposes of this chapter it provides a particularly good example of the situatedness of teaching in racialized contexts. It highlights the differences between the intended action and unintended consequences of teaching, and again establishes the role of teachers in the experiences of schooling and the politics of difference. However one interprets the debate, these issues of student–teacher interaction, the agency of teaching and the racialized contexts of teaching are central.

Teaching sexualities

The relationships between teaching, schooling and sexuality are vexed and multidimensional. Epstein and Johnson (1998) argue that sexuality is both dangerous and inescapable territory for teachers. There are various contexts in which sexuality and teaching interacts. There are statutory measures in place (such as section 28 of the 1988 Local Government Act in England which prohibits the 'promotion' of homosexuality by local authorities). Schools are charged with the task of providing sex education. The general press and educational media relish 'school' sex scandals and the 'outing' of educational actors. Also sexual identities are played out and learnt in school (Renold 2000) Hence, schooling and teaching are sexualized territories:

> In discourse, schools are constituted as public arenas, in contrast to the supposed private space of sexuality. Nevertheless schools are places where young people and their teachers do a great deal of cultural work on the construction of their identities in a whole range of ways, importantly, around issues of sexuality.
>
> (Epstein 1997: 106)

Beyond the formal requirements of sex education, sexualities are enmeshed in the everyday realities of schooling and, importantly, teaching. The identity work of the teacher is fundamentally tied to notions of sexuality. Indeed, teachers are desexualized in school contexts, and this must be married to the sexual realities of teacher selves. Teachers bear the primary responsibility for desexualizing schooling and for delivering sex education. Teachers serve as 'moral guardians', are responsible for regulating sexualities, must serve as role models *and* 'at the same time, teachers have, and indeed are expected to have, "exemplary" sexual lives outside the school. "Exemplary", in this context, entails being, ideally, heterosexual, married and, for women at least, with children who are already at school' (Epstein and Johnson 1998: 123). This has consequences for the identity work of all teachers, not just lesbian and gay teachers (see Chapter 5). This contradiction of desexualized schooling combined with the expectation of 'exemplary' sexuality also serves to deny the ways in which sexuality is enacted and embedded in school arenas, and in the everyday work of teaching. Epstein and Johnson argue that the surveillance of teachers in relation to sexuality is particularly strong in contemporary education systems, but that this follows a long-standing caution with teachers' sexualities (see Jones and Mahony 1989; Epstein 1994). However, the drive to erase sexuality from schools and to desexualize teachers has not been successful. Sexuality is part of the teacher identity, and also part of the discourse in which the teacher operates. For example, as Epstein and Johnson (1998) note, teachers frequently use sexual taunts to enforce their control. It could also be noted that teachers can be conceptualized as important agents of social change, with regard to challenging heterosexism and the desexualization of schooling (see Scott 1989; Coffey and Delamont 2000).

Conclusion

This chapter has focused on the work of teaching in contemporary and changing educational times. It is well recognized that teachers are at the sharp end of educational reforms, as the front-line providers of education. Hence, in addressing the changing contexts of education, the work and lives of teachers must remain a salient consideration. In the course of this chapter the lot of the teacher has been contextualized in a number of ways. The everyday work of the classroom teacher has been set alongside the social and cultural contexts of teaching. Teacher education and training provides a particularly striking example of the reformulation of relationships between the state, the teaching profession and teaching as work. All of this has been set within the broader frameworks of educational and school change. Throughout this chapter, and earlier ones, data from sociological research on education has been extensively drawn upon, and some research issues outlined. The next chapter takes research as its primary focus, locating the sociology of education within wider and shifting methodological debates and discourses.

8 (Re)defining educational research

Introduction

A central concern of this volume has been to explore relationships between educational policy, educational experiences and social research. Empirical examples have been drawn in order to delineate the shifting processes and practices of education, and to relate these to wider aspects of social change. In this final substantive chapter the focus remains with social research, but shifts from a consideration of research data (or results) to questions of research practice, process and representation. Hence this chapter seeks to engage with some of the current methodological debates and innovations in social research, and consider their relevance to (sociological) research in educational arenas and contexts. The chapter is not intended to be a prescriptive summary of the range of methods and strategies available to the educational researcher. Nor is it a comprehensive overview of the state or potential of educational research (see Murphy 1996). Rather this chapter considers contemporary critiques, and some possible futures of educational research, set against a backdrop of changing policy agendas and expanding methodological horizons. These provide the chapter with an organizational framework. First the particular (policy) contexts of contemporary educational research are briefly described. This is followed by a discussion of some of the current critiques and controversies that surround the education research project. Third, action research is explored as a particular example of educational research practice. Action research has had a long history in educational work, and is useful in helping to articulate relationships between research, policy and practice. Lastly the chapter considers educational research in postmodern times.

Research, policy and experiences

The early 1990s brought both criticism and clarification for educational research. Located within broader concerns of the growing tenuous relationships between education and its theoretical disciplines (including sociology),

commentators (see Edwards 1990) increasingly characterized educational research as being of broadly two kinds: small-scale, practical, school-based efforts
on the one hand, and government-commissioned test developments and policy
evaluations on the other. In the midst of this, it became increasingly difficult
to identify funding for 'basic' research with a strong disciplinary and theoretical base (Coffey and Acker 1991). Whether or not one is persuaded by
such a characterization is a matter of preference (and dependent on personal
understandings of what research should look like). However, there is little
doubt that a substantial amount of sociologically informed research on education has increasingly tended toward 'policy' research of various kinds, concerned with documenting and evaluating recent educational reforms.

This work has been paralleled by small-scale, in-depth research on
particular educational experiences, influenced (though not exclusively) by
an increased popularity of qualitative methods *and* calls for the recognition
of diverse experiences and voices within educational arenas. Ozga (2000: 1)
has described policy research in education as 'contested terrain'. Ozga argues
that conceptualizations of policy are continually struggled over, and methodological claims subject to sustained critical scrutiny. 'There are no agreed
definitions of policy, and researchers who work in this area are of many
different types. They pursue the research that they do for different reasons,
and many define the most important problems in educational policy research in sharply contrasting ways' (Ozga 2000: 4). Ozga identifies two contrastive approaches to educational 'policy' research – the policy analysis
project and the social science project. While these are not hard and fast
categories, and are subject to considerable interpretation (especially since
the recent proliferation of policy research), they do offer a useful means of
categorizing alternate research strands. Ozga suggests that the policy analysis
project currently dominates work of this kind:

> There is, perhaps, a continuum . . . from the very direct engagement
> with policy . . . to the less action oriented engagement with understand-
> ing policy . . . the policy analysis project is more strongly orientated
> towards finding solutions than enlarging understanding.
>
> (Ozga 2000: 40)

In contrast the social science project is more concerned with understanding:

> The problem is 'defined' by the nature of existing theory, and the
> orientation is towards improving existing theory; that is, a better
> understanding of how things work. The orientation is towards the
> academic discipline . . . and the rules of the discipline, and its principles
> of enquiry, guide research practice, rather than a framework of strategic
> planning, requirements and possibilities.
>
> (Ozga 2000: 40)

While there are, of course, crossovers between describing, commenting,
understanding and evaluating, Ozga supports the view that policy analysis
has become the dominant form of (social) research (on education). Indeed,
significant criticism has been made of educational research that is perceived to
have failed to engage directly with policy agendas (Hillage *et al.* 1998; Tooley

and Darby 1998). A substantial amount of recent sociological work on education has hence been concerned with responding to policy agendas and developments. And to an extent such approaches have fitted well with political arithmetic models of the sociology of education, concerned with examining the ways in which education contributes to economic prosperity, social mobility and the democratic society (Halsey *et al.* 1997). However, sociological research on education has also been, and is, fundamentally concerned with *understanding* educational arenas and processes (Ball and Gewirtz 1997). This can include addressing the impacts and possibilities of policy, but also broader frameworks concerned with documenting social change and educational experiences. Hence the research concern with 'policy' has micro as well as macro connotations.

Relatively small-scale, schools-based research has maintained a momentum for addressing educational processes, understandings, experiences and biographies. Ethnographic work in educational settings has enabled the lived realities of policy to be explored, and has sought to make sense of the continuities as well as the changes to educational experiences. Biographical and narrative work (see Chapter 5) has also promoted versions of education that link education to the (re)production of identities. However, these kinds of sociological work in educational settings are not dominant, although they have attracted substantial controversy of late (Tooley and Darby 1998). Yet these relatively small-scale and predominantly qualitative studies have refocused the teaching and learning agendas of education by exploring the lived realities of educational arenas. In the next section these tensions are further explored, by examining some of the recent critiques of educational research. These are set within the wider disciplinary context of the sociology of education.

Critiques and controversies

Evaluation and critique of recent educational research has been of two distinct kinds. First there has been a sustained redefinition of the relationships between education and policy, primarily emerging from two commissioned reports (Hillage *et al.* 1998; Tooley and Darby 1998). Second, there has been internal debate over some areas of educational research and their methodological underpinnings. This has mainly, though not exclusively, focused on a critique of the claims and politics of qualitative research.

Educational research critiqued

In 1998 two reports on the current state of educational research were published. *Excellence in Research on Schools* (Hillage *et al.* 1998) was produced by the Institute of Employment Studies, and commissioned by the Department for Education and Employment (DfEE). Evidence was gathered from England in order to 'undertake an analysis of the direction, organization, funding, quality and impact of educational research, primarily in the schools field' (Hillage *et al.* 1998: ix). The DfEE asked the authors to make recommendations for the development of educational research – and that this be done according to a specified set of objectives – to include the practical value of research, relevance to policy, value for money and quality assurance. Hillage *et al.* (1998) undertook a variety of tasks. These included a review of research literature; interviews with 'stakeholders'; and gathering evidence from the research community, local education authorities and trade unions as well as conducting focus groups and interviews with teachers, educational advisors and school inspectors. The conclusions of the report were wide-ranging but essentially critical of the linkages between educational research, policy and practice. While examples of good practice were identified, the authors remained unconvinced about the clarity of dissemination and level of impact of educational research, as their conclusion indicates:

> Our overall conclusion is that actions and decisions of policy-makers and practitioners are insufficiently informed by research. Where the research does address policy-relevant and practical issues it tends to
> - be small scale and fails to generate findings that are reliable and generalizable;
> - be insufficiently based on existing knowledge and therefore capable of advancing understanding;
> - be presented in a form or medium that is largely inaccessible to a non-academic audience; and lack interpretation for a policy making or practitioner audience.
>
> This results at least in part from a research effort that is predominantly supply (i.e. researcher) driven. Furthermore, the research agenda tends to be backward rather than forward looking – following policy not prompting it.
>
> (Hillage *et al.* 1998: xi)

Stemming from these conclusions came a wide range of recommendations. These emphasized a need to strengthen and consolidate relationships between educational research, policy and practice. In addition they stressed a need to improve the overall quality of educational research.

The second report, *Educational Research: A Critique* (Tooley and Darby 1998), was commissioned by the Office for Standards in Education (Ofsted), and was in part a response to a criticism levelled at educational research by Hargreaves during an annual Teacher Training Agency lecture (Hargreaves 1996). During this lecture Hargreaves highlighted the disjuncture between research and practice in education, and argued that there was much 'frankly second-rate educational research that does not make a serious contribution to fundamental theory or knowledge' (Hargreaves 1996: 7). The Ofsted-commissioned study took on board these criticisms levelled specifically at educational research, as well as the parallel attack on sociological work on education made by the Chief Inspector of Schools for England (Woodhead 1998). Tooley (with Darby) undertook a detailed analysis of a sample of articles published in selected academic, educational journals, including the *British Journal of Sociology of Education*. The relationship between the report and Ofsted clearly locates Tooley's analysis within popular educational discourses of standards and quality in education. A primary task of the report was to assess the *quality* of educational research, as manifested in published journal articles. Tooley and Darby (1998) developed criteria for assessing their sample of articles, around the themes of contribution to theory and knowledge, coordination with other research, and reference to educational practice. The Tooley and Darby report was highly critical of the contributions of educational research to educational theory or practice. It also questioned the methodological and ideological contexts of much educational research (which forms part of a recurrent theme in Tooley's work – see Tooley 1997, 2000, and the discussion below). Journal articles in leading sociology and educational journals, and by leading educational researchers and scholars, were heavily criticized, largely on methodological and ideological grounds. Tooley's main analysis focused on only 47 articles, which could be perceived as a rather small sample for drawing such general conclusions. As a 'policy text' transmitting a 'policy message' (Ozga 2000: 33) the report raised doubts about the quality of contemporary educational research, and the relevance of educational research to educational practice. It also questioned the connectedness between the concerns of educational researchers, and the priorities of teacher training, classroom practice and schools. One implication of the report is 'that as currently practised, educational research is bad for teachers, especially teachers in the process of professional formation' (Ozga 2000: 35). Essentially the position of the report was that research which did not have direct relevance for the classroom practitioner was unsatisfactory (or at least that is an inference that can readily be drawn).

The criticisms levelled collectively by Hargreaves, Woodhead and Tooley have been particularly damning of sociological research, and many of the comments can be perceived as attacks on sociology as a discipline:

> A closer look at the scholars and texts attacked reveals that most of the targets are sociologists, criticized for using ideas from Weber, Durkheim, Bourdieu or Habermas. The technical vocabulary of the discipline, such as *habitus* and 'organic solidarity' is ridiculed in the writings of Woodhead and Tooley.
>
> (Delamont 2000: 103)

Interestingly, while the British Educational Research Association responded to these attacks, the British Sociological Association did not, even though some of the papers and projects most fiercely criticized were sociological. Delamont (2000) argues that this says much about the status of the sociology of education within the discipline of sociology generally:

> The position of sociologists of education in 1999 is akin to the position of women in 1969: useful as a labouring proletariat but not part of the governing class. A few individuals whose field is education have been elected to high office, but the bulk of the intellectual work produced by the majority is simply ignored . . . the elite authors simply ignore the intellectual product of the subspecialism.
>
> (Delamont 2000: 104)

Criticisms levelled at educational research as a whole have been matched by methodological debate within education research circles. Once again sociological work has featured heavily.

Internal methodological controversy

In recent years there have been a number of methodological debates and controversies, many located within sociologically informed research on education. These are in addition to the reports discussed above, and have focused on specific authors and research topics. Though not exclusively so, these controversies have been concerned with readdressing the claims and politics of qualitative research. For our purposes here, two debates are briefly discussed. One focuses on research on race and schooling (and expands the discussion of teaching and race in Chapter 7). The second considers methodological debate about research on markets in education and school choice.

The sociology of education has witnesed a series of exchanges focusing on relationships between research, methods, politics and equity. These mainly took place during the 1990s. At the centre has been a 'project of methodological criticism' (Gillborn 1995) advanced primarily by Peter Foster, Roger Gomm and Martyn Hammersley (see Foster 1990, 1992, 1993; Hammersley and Gomm 1993, 1996; Foster *et al.* 1996; Foster and Hammersley 1998; see also Chapter 7 of this volume). Between them these scholars have been responsible for a cumulative and critical attack on some sociological research on race and education, advanced by Gillborn and colleagues (see Gillborn 1995, 1998). This cumulative critique targeted 'research that claims to have identified some of the processes by which racism is implicated in the patterning of racial disadvantage in schools' (Gillborn 1995: 51). A target of this criticism has been some educational researchers, and the ways in which they have made claims about racial educational inequalities based on their research findings. A main claim of Foster and his colleagues is that many of the qualitative studies of racial injustice in school fail to stand up to sustained methodological scrutiny. They have argued that these researchers have brought to their research political agendas that have coloured their analysis, and that the evidence does not support their claims of racialized inequalities and racism in schools.

In subjecting a number of empirical investigations on race and schooling to critical review, Foster, Hammersley and Gomm have been accused of methodological purism (see Troyna 1993b). As Gillborn and Troyna have both noted, this translates into a debate about proving a case beyond reasonable doubt. Hammersley (1993), however, has attempted to outline his position. He rejects the label of purism in favour of methodological common sense, and argues 'all claims and evidence must be judged on the basis of two considerations: plausibility in relation to knowledge we currently take as beyond reasonable doubt, and credibility in relation to judgements about the likelihood of various sorts of error' (Hammersley 1993: 340).

However, the failure to prove the case of racism within schools beyond reasonable doubt, combined with the potential built-in errors of the researchers, serve as cornerstones of this critique launched by Foster, Hammersley and Gomm. They found commonalities in the research strategies and political motivations of the researchers under scrutiny, and equated political motivation (anti-racism) with the potential of partiality in research. Accordingly they have argued that political motivations, however well intended, can lead to compromise for the researcher, and can question the scholastic rigour of the research.

This debate has centred on questions of rigour, validity and truth. It pivots on a disjuncture between Foster's own work on race and education (Foster 1990), in which racism of teachers and the school was not highlighted as a major issue despite race differences in the school, and other work in the field (for example that of Wright 1986; Mac an Ghaill 1988; Gillborn 1990). This critical reading – especially with regard to the lack of evidence of teacher racism – is understood in terms of partiality, political motivation and the non-rigorous interpretation of evidence.

Gillborn, in particular, has been highly critical of the stance taken by Foster and his colleagues, not least because his own work has held centre stage in the debate. Gillborn (1995: 55) defends the right of scholars to critique educational research but takes issue with the consequences of the criticisms:

> The 'methodological purists' have every right to be critical of research. The main problem with their project lies in its persistent attempt not only to raise problems, but to go beyond this, to conclude that there are no good reasons to believe that minority students are initially disadvantaged by school based processes and the actions of teachers.

Gillborn hence concludes that the methodological project advanced by Foster and his colleagues may actually play a role in defending and sustaining existing racial inequalities (but see Hammersley 1993: 340 who argues that a response such as this 'undercuts the basis for productive discussion and virtually rules out the possibility of reaching agreement'):

> It reduces institutional racism to the status of a mere theoretical possibility . . . privilege(s) the status quo . . . produces a static and deeply conservative notion of social science [and] embodies a conception of science that is blind to all but the most crude operations of power and politics. By denying that scientific discourse is itself implicated in the processes of cultural production and reproduction, the 'methodological purists' offer a presumption for sociology that is at best ethnocentric, at worst racist.
>
> (Gillborn 1995: 63)

This particular methodological controversy revolves around squaring political stance with empirical research, and the generalization of evidence. While not explicitly criticizing qualitative methods or ethnography *per se*, the debate is set within the parameters of establishing proof over interpretation, and denying the personal and political nature of research and its consequences. This echoes a more general debate over the place of reflexivity in research, and the position of the researcher (see Coffey 1999). The sustained critique of research on social class and school choice demonstrates similar tensions. This is briefly discussed below.

Qualitative investigations into social class and school choice have been one of the areas considered by James Tooley (1997, 2000; see also Tooley and Darby 1998). He has specifically focused on the work of Ball and his colleagues, and has framed his critique in terms of methodological challenge although, as Ozga (2000: 65) notes, this also serves as a 'proxy for his disagreement with their view of the market'. The research on school choice and social class, about which Tooley (1997: 217) calls the work of Ball, Bowe and Gewirtz 'perhaps the most important published research' (see Bowe *et al.* 1994; Ball *et al.* 1995, 1996; Gewirtz *et al.* 1995; see also comparable work on school choice and social class: David *et al.* 1994; Waslander and Thrupp 1995; Thrupp 1999), establishes and explores the relationships between educational markets and social class. As Ball and Gewirtz (1997: 577) note, 'our main concern . . . was to explore the nature and complexity of the relationship and the processes involved in the reproduction of social class advantage through the market form'.

The qualitative study on school choice undertaken by Gewirtz, Ball and Bowe concentrated on interviews with key social actors (including parents) in three local educational authorities in London. In documenting the processes and outcomes of school choice, Gewirtz *et al.* revealed the class modes of social engagement, and the ways in which social class shaped and increasingly segregated school provision. Hence their study has made a substantial contribution to the work on social inequalities and school markets. Tooley (1997) has attacked this work, primarily focusing on the methodological approach, and the consequent conclusions that they felt able to draw. In short, Tooley disputes the ability of qualitative research to provide evidence to support the conclusions which Gewirtz *et al.* (and indeed others) have drawn. Tooley limits the potential of qualitative research to provide anecdotal, or example, data, rather than main data from which conclusions can usefully be drawn. In commenting specifically on their choice of approach Tooley (1997: 220) states that

> there is a clear need and value for this kind of qualitative work; to give us further insights into the school choice process. But while eschewing statistical methods is certainly legitimate, it does then put constraints on what can be reported as research findings.

Tooley's methodological challenge to Gewirtz and her colleagues culminates in the conclusion that their empirical evidence does not support a sustainable case against markets in education. Tooley (1997) identifies his approach as fitting into the same normative framework as Foster and colleagues (see above), and makes a number of specific criticisms of the project, for example that generalizations cannot (should not) be drawn from (small-scale) qualitative research; that the sample size constitution and locale (London) of the research were insufficient and unrepresentative; that the longitudinal nature of the research did not take into account shifting and evolving policy contexts. While these are particular criticisms (to which Ball and Gewirtz 1997 have responded in detail), Tooley is also engaged on a more general project. He re-establishes a dichotomy between qualitative and quantitative research, whereby qualitative data provides human colour and illustrative instances, and not data that are 'objective' and generalizable. Moreover, Tooley argues that the ideological convictions of the researchers skewed their analysis and data interpretation, a point which he reaffirms in later writings; 'choice in education seems too much tied up with a discredited ideology, with unpalatable implications for education' (Tooley 2000: 125).

In their response to Tooley, Ball and Gewirtz (1997) deal with both the specific criticisms of their particular project (issues of locale, sample, generalization) and the broader methodological critique. They justify their methodological decision making, and the general conclusions that they felt able to draw. Aside from these particular points (and recognizing that it is perfectly valid for research projects to undergo scrutiny), Ball and Gewirtz engage with the wider implications of what Tooley is arguing. As an attack on qualitative research *and* political, ideologically involved research, they argue that Tooley's approach is fundamentally flawed. At the heart is a misunderstanding of the nature, procedures and canons of qualitative research, and the potential of this to explore the nature and complexities of educational relationships and processes:

> Tooley's discussion of the possibilities of generalization are tortuous and confusing. He sees qualitative research as a valid means of access to 'process of choice' but appears to want a different type and style of research to achieve 'generalizable' findings – he constantly uses such terms without clear specification. There is some vague but unarticulated sense of a sample size that would allow 'generalizations' to be made. There is a naïve positivism at work somewhere here.
>
> (Ball and Gewirtz 1997: 580)

Ball and Gewirtz point to a plethora of research on school choice and social class, and argue that, while caricaturing their work, Tooley also ignores other research that serves to triangulate and confirm their findings. On the point of ideology/positions, Ball and Gewirtz reveal Tooley to be caught up in his own critique. Tooley is a keen advocate of the educational market place and school choice, and hence 'it would be naïve to disconnect Tooley's methodological concerns from the advocacy of choice in his other writings' (Ball and Gewirtz 1997: 577). Thus Tooley's critique can be recast in terms of methodological and ideological positioning, based on different assumptions about research, and a rather different view of the social world and his own personal political agenda (Ball and Gewirtz 1997).

The two debates I have outlined here are both projects of methodological criticism, but are also tied up with the ideological and theoretical positioning of research. Both sets of critiques seek to mount challenges to the possibilities of qualitative research, and argue for a kind of methodological purism, divorced from social theory and political stance. At the same time, it can be demonstrated that the critics themselves are involved in utilizing social research and methodological standpoints as mechanisms for pursuing their own agendas and views of the social (and educational) worlds. Educational research has been, and continues to be, the site for scrutiny and debate. The dialogues that I have outlined indicate the ways in which educational research is located within broader methodological 'conversations' about (for example) relationships between research, policy and practice, and questions of politics, validity and evidence. These themes are followed through in the next section of this chapter, which explores the action research as a recurrent educational research model.

Educational research as action research

Action research was described by Cohen and Manion (1980: 174) as 'a small scale intervention in the functioning of the real world and close examination of the effects of such intervention'. In other words action research refers to a kind of research which sets in train some changes in a setting, and then seeks to monitor the progress and effects of such change (Carr and Kemmis 1986; Noffke and Stevenson 1995). This kind of research, grounded in collaboration between researcher and practitioner, has played a significant part in the educational research enterprise. Fundamentally it has involved teachers as researchers (Elliott and Sarland 1995), analysts and the catalysts for change. Teachers-as-researchers, through an action research model, have been responsible for researching their own practice and for enacting change in schools (Day 1995; Donald *et al.* 1995; Frost 1995). Action research projects can take a number of forms – and involve teachers to differing degrees. Some aim to work *with* teachers. Others are more explicit in making teachers the researchers, as a means of developing a collaborative approach. In doing so, action research attempts to bridge the gap between research and practice:

> It directly addresses the knotty problem of the persistent failure of research in the social sciences to make a difference in terms of bringing about actual improvements in practice. It does so by rejecting the concept of a two-stage process in which research is carried out first by researchers and then in a separate stage the knowledge generated is applied by practitioners. Instead the two processes of research and action are integrated.
>
> (Somekh 1995: 340)

Educational action research is an attempt to integrate research with the development of educational practice, and has a long history (see Stenhouse 1975; Elliott 1991). Primarily geared toward the development of teaching practice, it is a model of research foreshadowed in initial and in-service teacher education, and is perhaps the central way in which educational practitioners have engaged in the everyday rigours of (sociological) research. Action research has also been used as a model in the development of knowledge, involving schools and universities in participatory collaboration. There have been a number of attempts to chart the methodological underpinnings and experiences of action research. The collection edited by Atweh *et al.* (1998) presents a series of case studies of the action research tradition in Australia. These stress the political and social justice underpinnings of the action research model, and the centrality of cooperation between researchers, teachers and institutions. The special issue of the *British Educational Research Journal* (1995: 21(3)) particularly addressed the questions of empowerment in teacher research, and was strengthened by the inclusion of accounts from teachers of their own action research experiences. For example, Chiswell (1995) reflected on her involvement in action research, and the ways in which this contributed to the development of her role as communicator within the school, as well as challenging her teaching practice. 'This course of study has required me to examine and reflect upon my teaching in a critical way, to analyse my strengths and weaknesses, and by implementing action steps, provide the means of altering or improving my teaching practices' (Chiswell 1995: 413).

An area where action research has been particularly influential has been in the field of gender and education. Action research here highlights these political and social dimensions and the value of collaboration and cooperation (see also Donald *et al.* 1995 and Ryan 1995 for accounts of action research in multinational contexts). Action research has been a mainstay of small-scale research on gender and education and has been a source and site of collaboration between feminist academics, teachers and other educational workers. Work in secondary schools (Kelly 1985; Whyte 1986; Burchall and Millman 1989; McKinnon and Ahola-Sidaway 1995) has been matched by work in nursery and primary education (see for example Browne and France 1986). Action research has been carried out with girls (Weiner 1985; Quicke and Winter 1995) and with boys (Askew and Ross 1988; Jackson and Salisbury 1996). Sexuality and sex education has also provided a particular focus for action research initiatives (Holly 1989; Jones and Mahony 1989; Epstein 1994).

Teachers themselves have been instrumental in the development and practical application of action research, and in many cases have navigated the boundary between teacher and researcher. May and Ruddock (1983) reported on a project in Norfolk, England, which gave early years teachers the opportunity to become independent researchers. Teachers were encouraged and helped to design and conduct their own investigations into the gender dynamics of their own schools. One of the best-known examples of the action research model in the UK is the GIST project – Girls into Science and Technology – which ran in the early 1980s (Whyte 1987). Here researchers worked alongside and with teachers, as opposed to adopting a teacher-as-researcher model. Academic researchers worked with the full range of teachers in 10 Manchester schools – and implemented a set of innovations designed to encourage young women to persevere with 'male' craft and science subjects, after they became optional rather than compulsory curriculum subjects (then at age 14 years). The team brought adult women working as scientists and technicians into the schools to act as role models, raised the consciousness of the teachers about the gender dynamics of classrooms, and experimented with teaching maths and science to single sex classes in co-educational schools. The reports on GIST (Kelly 1985; Whyte 1986) highlighted that one of the main difficulties of the project was the teachers. Choosing to attempt to work with the full range of teachers meant working with teachers (mostly men) who were unsympathetic to the aims of the project and explicitly anti-feminist. Other projects in the UK – such as the Girls and Technology education project (GATE) and Girls and Occupational Choice (GAOC) opted for closer collaboration with teachers – relying on volunteer teachers (already sympathetic to the cause). However these projects, too, were not without problems (see Chisholm and Holland 1987).

Stronach and MacLure (1997) report on the 'teachers as researchers' project in the UK that aimed to study teacher action research. The project included life history interviews with key actors of the British teacher-centred action research movement. They highlight that teachers who move into action research, often through a process of leaving teaching, face a number of oppositional dilemmas

> between theory and practice; between the personal and the professional; between the organizational cultures of the social and the academy; between 'insider' and 'outsider' perspectives; between the sacred language of science, scholarship or research, and the mundane dialects of practice and everyday experience.
>
> (Stronach and MacLure 1997: 116–17)

In Stronach and MacLure's terms, action research is a 'boundary dweller', pasted between research and teaching, theory and practice. A key transition for teacher action researchers is often the withdrawing from teaching, and the 'exit' work that this entails. Teachers who move full-time into research face the difficulties of 'exiting' from teaching and 'entering' into the world of research, while at the same time needing to maintain synergy between the two. For as Stronach and MacLure (1997: 128–9) argue, action research has

> drawn its power (and also, of course, its problems of legitimation within the institutional discourse of theory and research) from its challenge to the customary dispositions of 'privilege' in the unequal relations of dualism – between theory and practice, subjectivity and objectivity, academic and practitioner. It has developed a powerful critique of the academic discourse of positivist science and scholarship, and the tyrannies that theory and expertise have exacted upon the teacher as the *Other*.

The concept of the teacher-as-researcher is related to the familiar concept of the teacher-as-reflective-practitioner (Schon 1983, 1987; Zeichner and Liston 1987; Gore and Zeichner 1991; Valli 1992; Frost 1995; James 1996). Teacher education has routinely been concerned with engaging student teachers in exercises of reflection, and in the development of reflexive practice (Stenhouse 1975; Harrington *et al.* 1996; Wade and Yarborough 1996). This has come under increasing pressure within the new regimes of teacher education (Maguire 1995). Together the concepts of action research and the reflective practitioner encompass what Stanley (1990) has called research *praxis* which she describes as a commitment to change, a rejection of the conventional dualisms of theory and practice, and the velocity of research to the production of knowledge. This has been particularly embraced in feminist articulations of educational research praxis. For example Weiner (1994: 130) develops a view of educational research which is

- deriving from experience and rooted in practice;
- continually subject to revision as a result of experience;
- reflexive and self-reflexive;
- widely accessible and open to change;
- grounded in the analysis of women's (and men's) multiple and different experiences and material values;
- explicitly political and value-led;
- within the classroom; imbued with feminist organizational practices grounded in equality, non-hierarchy and democracy;

- within educational research, additionally rejecting conventional dualisms, such as theory/practice, mental/manual, epistemology/methodology.

Action research can be seen as one response to criticisms that educational research is often not practitioner-relevant, although ironically action research projects are often small-scale (and qualitative), grounded in personal experiences and ongoing processes of reflection, and linked to political (social justice) agendas. Somekh (1995) has argued that action research challenges the assumptions and status of traditional research, and hence has been subjected to some attack. She also suggests that the rise in postmodern perspectives (and the methodological implications of these) 'has made it much easier to present action research as a serious research methodology, without apology' (Somekh 1995: 347). It is to the relationships between postmodernism and (educational) research that this chapter now turns.

Educational research with/in the postmodern

Contemporary sociological research is infused with debates over the relationships between social research and calls toward postmodernism and post-structuralism. Stronach and MacLure (1997) discuss the postmodern discourse and practice in educational research, and offer models of what postmodernist educational research might look like (see also special issue of *British Educational Research Journal*, 1995. 22(3)). Stronach and MacLure recognize the inherent difficulty in offering a single view of research in the face of a postmodern diversity, and argue for seeing the value in embracing the approaches and perspectives that are potentially offered by postmodern perspectives:

> Educational engagements with postmodernism exhibit the same kind of anxiety, and the same kinds of attempts to contain or circumscribe its dangers, that have recurred in every other field or discipline that has courted its embrace. On the one hand, poststructuralism and deconstruction offer valuable resources for exposing the complicity of language in the workings of reality, society, power, knowledge and identity ... On the other hand, educational writings display the same kinds of 'fearful conditionals', the same uncertainty as to whether it is a poison or a remedy, that are found in other fields.
>
> (Stronach and MacLure 1997: 7–8)

In attempting to articulate the spaces offered by postmodernism and post-structuralism Stronach and MacLure present new ways of thinking about research design, analysis and, importantly, representation – suggesting that educational research needs to address the issues and opportunities put forward by (post-)feminism and post-colonialism; globalization; the reformulation of identities; and the challenges to mainstream conventional disciplines (such as literary studies, anthropology, philosophy and sociology):

> Political surrenders are familiar enough to us now and we need a kind of cultural revolution in educational research, not in favour of some kind of new orthodoxy, but in favour of experiment, creativity and

risk. To those who confine themselves to the politics of nostalgia, we would say that mourning that loss (of certainty, 'science', 'enlightenment', 'ideas' or 'autonomy') is a necessary thing, especially if it constitutes the double loss of something that never existed. But it should not become a way of life. Life goes on and with it, perhaps, even, sometimes, if we are creative enough, persistent enough, a sharper and less compliant educational research.

(Stronach and MacLure, 1997: 152)

The relationships between postmodern (post-structural, post-feminist) perspectives and social science research have been particularly well articulated and debated by those working within qualitative paradigms. Lincoln and Denzin (1994), for example, in their authoritative review identify a narrative periodization of the development of qualitative research – from positivist and modernist movements – through multiplicity and crisis – to diversity and a series of tensions:

Qualitative research embraces two tensions at the same time. On the one hand, it is drawn to a broad, interpretative, post-modern, feminist, and critical sensibility. On the other hand, it can also be drawn to more narrowly defined positivist, post-positivist, humanistic and naturalistic conceptions of human experience and its analysis.

(Lincoln and Denzin 1994: 576)

Lincoln and Denzin characterize a future of qualitative research suffused with reflexive, experimental texts that are messy, subjective, open-ended, conflictual and feminist-influenced (Lincoln and Denzin 1994: 559). The narrative periodization offered by Denzin and Lincoln has been criticized as being overly rigid (Coffey 1999), and less than satisfactory for conceptualizing qualitative research in education (Delamont *et al.* 2000). The majority of qualitative researchers in education have done little to engage with the radical, diverse and experimental approaches to research and representation offered by Denzin and Lincoln's model of contemporary ethnography. Indeed, at best, qualitative researchers in education have been slow to adopt textual and other innovations compared to ethnographers in other fields, such as science (see Mulkay 1985) and health (Bluebond-Langer 1980; Paget 1993). The moves toward a more critical appreciation of the production of research texts and the implication of multiple voices and multiple selves in (and in the authoring of) research are, however, important identifications to be made. More so than ever before we are aware of the 'craft skills' of writing and representing research. This is encapsulated in the burgeoning of texts on how to write and read research (Hammersley 1991; Atkinson 1996; Ely *et al.* 1997; Richardson 2000). A more self-conscious approach to writing has been encouraged (for example in texts such as Ely *et al.* 1997), exploring and understanding how we compose meaning from our data and how we make our data meaningful to others. At the very least, writing and representing research are no longer taken for granted aspects of the research process. The articulation of the self in the products of research has also become a matter of critical reflection. Relationships between the research process, the writing process and the self have reconceptualized the emotional and personal dimensions of research, and drawn attention to issues of authorship and authenticity (Coffey 1996). 'Authors' are no longer all-but 'invisible'. Conventional texts, as research texts, have been criticized for not doing justice to the multi- or polyvocality of social life and social forms.

In practice, the impact of such articulations on the written products of social research has been peripheral rather than central to the social science research endeavour, including within educational research (Delamont et al. 2000). Some new representational forms have been proposed and experimented with, in order to reflect the general postmodernist agenda of how research is translated into representations and forms of knowledge production. This can be seen as being especially significant to the feminist concern with the production and representation of knowledges. Feminists have questioned conventional styles of writing and representing (Wolf 1992), and feminist epistemology has challenged conventional forms of scholarly narrative as masculinist (Behar and Gordon 1995). Attempts to transform the researcher's position of privilege and 'undo' the conventions of academic scholarship production have challenged the conventional textual formats of scholarly writing (as exemplified in the collection edited by Ellis and Bochner 1996, and described by Ely et al. 1997). Alternative genres have included scripts, poetry, performance texts, diaries, and collaborative writing. Many draw on a dialogic approach to text (Dwyer 1977; Holquist 1990; Allan 1994), and promote a self-conscious (auto)biographical approach to writing (Mykhalovskiy 1997; Coffey 1999; Ellis and Bochner 2000). They exemplify the relationships between social research and the production and writing of selves and lives (Hastrup 1992; Stanley 1992).

While scripts, dialogues, poetry and similar genres have not been used extensively within educational research there are notable examples. McCoy's (1997) use of poetry as a way of exploring pre-service teachers' use of the discourses of cultural difference is a particularly striking and seductive way of presenting what would otherwise be potentially difficult arguments and ideas. Stronach and MacLure (1997) write some of their text as messy text – with reader/author dialogue, footnotes and text notes interwoven into the text – which is presented in different columns on the page. Middleton (1995) also experiments with her writing in a piece on feminist educational theory, writing in two columns to represent the academic and the personal voice. The *International Journal of Qualitative Studies in Education* has published a number of experimental educational texts: see for example the poetry of Torres (1997) and Retana (1998), and the narrative of Gray (1998).

Collaborative approaches to textual production and the writing of research are another distinctive and innovative way in which representation is challenged and reconfigured in postmodern times. Collaboration has always been a feature of feminist and action research. The work by Haw on educating Muslim girls (1998) is an exemplary example of a feminist collaborative approach to the writing (and researching) task within educational research. The text is collaboratively authored by Haw (a white, non-Muslim researcher), Shab (a Muslim, Pakistani woman, and head of a tertiary college in Pakistan) and Hanifa (a woman Muslim teacher in one of the school settings of the research). The text contains conversations and dialogues, personal reflections, (auto)biographical notes, responses and alternative visions. Crucially it provides a view of research which (cautiously) celebrates polyvocality and the (auto)biographical. Creative approaches to the production of research texts can aid and promote a reflexive and self-conscious approach to textual production and the creation of knowledge. Some, like Sparkes (1995), argue that they create the opportunity for more realistic pictures of events, and serve to blur the power boundaries between researcher and researched. This is not, however, a universally agreed view, even by those who have engaged in and practised different modes of representation. Lather (1991), for example, has argued that alternative representative forms do not remove the issue of power from the production of research. Texts are still authored – and selected, collected, edited, presented, written, crafted and read. As such, alternative forms of writing may blur or question boundaries but do not remove the issues. Indeed, the very artfulness of many alternative or experiential texts actually draws attention to the craft work of authorship. Ethno-drama, theatrical scripts and poetry serve to emphasize the creative potential and power of the author by overtly manipulating the appearance and ordering of words and text. By foregrounding the researcher as author, they could be conceptualized as a means of increasing, rather than diminishing, the distance between researcher and other. Equally, such textual practice exposes the researcher-as-author to new forms of critical scrutiny. In dealing with critiques about authority and authorship by presenting new forms of representation, such practices expose the researcher to not only 'getting it right' as a social researcher, and scriptor of social life, but also as a more or less successful poet, playwright or creative writer.

Despite the limited use of postmodern and post-structural approaches to the tasks of researching and (re)presenting education, they do 'constitute a way of looking at the world which [educational] researchers are increasingly finding useful' (Paechter and Weiner 1996: 271). Such approaches do not constitute in themselves a singular research method, but do present analytical frameworks for developing and rethinking educational research, for example by offering wider visions of discourse and representation, a refocusing on the local, and alternative perspectives for viewing the social world. Hence it becomes possible to 'liberate existing research practice, making way for a diversity of perspectives and voices, and a complexity of research outcomes' (Paechter and Weiner 1996: 271).

Conclusion

Sociological investigations of contemporary education have furthered our understanding of the processes, outcomes and experiences of educational arenas and policies. They have also been influential in locating this understanding within broader conceptualizations of social change. As this chapter has illustrated, educational research has also provided the site for ongoing methodological debate and innovation. Theoretical development and the widening of the substantial remit of what counts as education (Burgess 1986) has been paralleled by a growing interest in the ways in which we 'come to know' and write about these educational processes, outcomes and experiences. While the sociology of education has been relatively slow to embrace some of the new and innovative methodological practices, the field has prompted an increasing amount of methodological discussion. This reflects an increasing trend within sociology to reflect upon the craft skills of the discipline, making explicit the ways to data, as well as the meanings of those data. More generally it reflects the enhanced role of reflexivity in contemporary sociological discussion. This process of questioning and examining social science knowledge (and indeed the social scientist) does not render the sociological project meaningless. Rather it recognizes the recursive relationships between social knowledge, society and social change. This book has primarily been concerned with documenting contemporary education, in a context of social and economic change. There is a parallel story to be told – understanding the sociology of education in the context of the discipline of sociology, and theoretical, substantive and methodological challenges of the new century.

References

Acker, S. (ed.) (1989) *Teachers, Gender and Careers*. Lewes: Falmer.

Acker, S. (1994) *Gendered Education: Sociological Reflections on Women, Teaching and Feminism*. Buckingham: Open University Press.

Adams, K. and Emery, K. (1994) 'Classroom coming out stories: Practical strategies for productive self disclosure', in L. Garber (ed.) *Tilting the Tower: Lesbians/Teaching/Queer Subject*. New York, NY: Routledge.

Agar, M. (1986) Foreword to T.L. Whitehead and M.E. Conway (eds) *Self, Sex and Gender in Cross-Cultural Fieldwork*. Urbana, IL: University of Illinois Press.

Allan, S. (1994) '"When discourse is torn from reality": Bakhtin and the principle of chronologoplicity', *Time and Society*, 3, 193–218.

Apple, M. (ed.) (1982) *Cultural and Economic Reproduction in Education*. London: Routledge.

Apple, M. (1986) *Teachers and Texts: A Political Economy of Class and Gender Relations in Education*. New York, NY: Routledge and Kegan Paul.

Apple, M. (1998) 'Education and the new hegemonic blocs: Doing policy the "right" way', *International Studies in Sociology of Education*, 8(2), 181–202.

Apple, M.W. (1997) 'What postmodernists forget: Cultural capital and official knowledge', in A.H. Halsey, H. Lauder, P. Brown and A. Stuart Wells (eds) *Education: Culture, Economy, Society*. Oxford: Oxford University Press (first published 1993, *Curriculum Studies*, 1, 301–16).

Arnot, M., David, M. and Weiner, G. (1996) *Educational Reforms and Gender Equality in Schools*. Manchester: Equal Opportunities Commission.

Arnot, M., David, M. and Weiner, G. (1999) *Closing the Gender Gap: Postwar Education and Social Change*. Cambridge: Polity Press.

Arnot, M., Gray, J., James, M., Rudduck, J. with Duveen, G. (1998) *Recent Research on Gender and Educational Performance*. London: Ofsted/HMSO.

Arnot, M. and Weiler, K. (eds) (1993) *Feminism and Social Justice in Education*. London: Falmer.

Askew, S. and Ross, C. (eds) (1988) *Boys Don't Cry: Boys and Sexism in Education*. Milton Keynes: Open University Press.

Atkinson, P.A. (1996) *Sociological Readings and Re-readings*. Aldershot: Avebury.

Atkinson, P. and Silverman, D. (1997) 'Kundera's *Immortality*: The interview society and the invention of the self', *Qualitative Inquiry*, 3(3), 304–25.

Attar, D. (1990) *Wasting Girls' Time: The History and Politics of Home Economics*. London: Virago.

Atweh, B., Kemmis, S. and Weeks, P. (1998) *Action Research in Practice*. London and New York, NY: Routledge.

Avis, J. (1995) 'Post-compulsory education: Curricular forms, modernization and social difference', *International Studies in Sociology of Education*, 5(1), 57–76.

Bailey, L. (1996) 'The feminization of a school? Women teachers in a boys' school', *Gender and Education*, 8(2), 171–84.

Ball, S.J. (1981) *Beachside Comprehensive: A Case Study of Comprehensive Schooling*. Cambridge: Cambridge University Press.

Ball, S.J. (1990) *Politics and Policy Making in Education: Explorations in Policy Sociology*. London: Routledge.

Ball, S.J. (1993) 'Education markets, choice and social class: The market as a class strategy in the UK and USA', *British Journal of Sociology of Education*, 14(1), 3–19.

Ball, S.J. (1994) *Education Reform: A Critical and Post-Structural Approach*. Buckingham: Open University Press.

Ball, S.J. (1997) 'Good school/bad school: Paradox and fabrication', *British Journal of Sociology of Education*, 18(3), 317–36.

Ball, S.J., Bowe, R. and Gewirtz, S. (1995) 'Circuits of schooling: A sociological exploration of parental choice of school in social class contexts', *Sociological Review*, 43, 52–78.

Ball, S.J., Bowe, R. and Gewirtz, S. (1996) 'School choice, social class and distinction: The realization of social advantage in education', *Journal of Education Policy*, 11, 89–112.

Ball, S.J. and Gewirtz, S. (1997) 'A rejoinder to Tooley's "On school and social class"', *British Journal of Sociology of Education*, 18(4), 575–86.

Ball, S.J. and Vincent, C. (1998) '"I heard it on the grapevine": "Hot" knowledge and school choice', *British Journal of Sociology of Education*, 19(3), 377–400.

Banks, O. (1981) *Faces of Feminism: A Study of Feminism as a Social Movement*. Oxford: Martin Robertson.

Beck, E.T. (1994) 'Out as a lesbian, out as a Jew: And nothing untoward happened', in L. Garber (ed.) *Tilting the Tower: Lesbians/Teaching/Queer Subject*. New York, NY: Routledge.

Beck, J. (1996) 'Citizenship education: Problems and possibilities', *Curriculum Studies*, 4(3), 349–66.

Beck, U. (1992) *Risk Society*. London: Sage.

Behar, R. and Gordon, D. (eds) (1995) *Women Writing Culture*. Berkeley, CA: University of California Press.

Bell, C. and Chase, S. (1993) 'The underrepresentation of women in school leadership', in C. Marshall (ed.) *The New Politics of Race and Gender*. Washington, DC: Falmer.

Bell, C. and Encel, S. (eds) (1978) *Inside the Whale: Ten Personal Accounts of Social Research*. Oxford: Pergamon.

Benhabib, S. (1995) 'Feminism and post-modernism: An uneasy alliance', in S. Benhabib, J. Butler, D. Cornell and N. Fraser (eds) *Feminist Contentions: A Philosophical Exchange*. New York, NY: Routledge.

Berliner, D. and Biddle, B.J. (1995) *The Manufactured Crisis*. New York, NY: Longman.

Bernstein, B. (1971) 'On the classification and framing of educational knowledge', in M.F.D. Young (ed.) *Knowledge and Control: New Directions for the Sociology of Education*. London: Macmillan.

Bernstein, B. (1975) *Class, Codes and Control, Volume 3: Towards a Theory of Educational Transmissions*. London: Routledge and Kegan Paul.

Bernstein, B. (1990) *Class, Codes and Control, Volume 5: The Structuring of Pedagogic Discourse*. London: Routledge.

Beynon, J. (1989) 'A school for men', in S. Walker and L. Barton (eds) *Politics and Processes of Schooling*. Milton Keynes: Open University Press.

Biddle, B.J., Good, T.L. and Goodson, I.F. (1997) 'The changing world of teachers', in B.J. Biddle, T.L. Good and I.F. Goodson (eds) *International Handbook of Teachers and Teaching*. Dordrecht: Kluwer.

Billington, R., Hockey, J. and Strawbridge, S. (1998) *Exploring Self and Society*. London: Macmillan.

Blackmore, J. (1999) *Troubling Women: Feminism, Leadership and Educational Change*. Buckingham: Open University Press.

Blair, M. and Holland, J. (with S. Sheldon) (eds) (1995) *Identity and Diversity: Gender and the Experience of Education*. Clevedon: Multilingual Matters (in association with The Open University).

Blinick, B. (1994) 'Out in the curriculum, out in the classroom: Teaching history and organizing for change', in L. Garber (ed.) *Tilting the Tower: Lesbians/Teaching/Queer Subject*. New York, NY: Routledge.

Bluebond-Langer, M. (1980) *The Private Worlds of Dying Children*. Princeton, NJ: Princeton University Press.

Boulton, P. and Coldron, J. (1998) 'Why women say "stuff it" to promotion', *Gender and Education*, 10(2), 149–62.

Bourdieu, P. (1993) *The Field of Cultural Production: Essays on Art and Literature*. Cambridge: Polity Press.

Bourdieu, P. and Passerson, J.C. (1977) *Reproduction in Education and Society*. London: Sage.

Bowe, R., Ball, S.J. and Gewirtz, S. (1994) 'Captured by the discourse? Issues and concerns in researching "parental choice"', *British Journal of Sociology of Education*, 15, 63–58.

Broadfoot, P. (1998) 'Quality standards and control in higher education: What price life-long learning?', *International Studies in Sociology of Education*, 8(2), 155–81.

Brodribb, S. (1992) *Nothing Mat(t)ers: A Feminist Critique of Postmodernism*. Melbourne: Spinifex Press.

Brown, P. (1990) 'The "third wave": Education and the ideology of parentocracy', *British Journal of Sociology of Education*, 11, 65–85.

Brown, P. (1997) 'The "third wave": Education and the ideology of parentocracy', in A.H. Halsey, H. Lauder, P. Brown and A. Stuart Wells (eds) *Education: Culture, Economy, Society*. Oxford: Oxford University Press.

Brown, P., Halsey, A.H., Lauder, H. and Wells, A. Stuart (1997) 'The transformation of education and society: An introduction', in A.H. Halsey, H. Lauder, P. Brown and A. Stuart Wells (eds) *Education: Culture, Economy, Society*. Oxford: Oxford University Press.

Browne, N. and France, P. (1986) *Untying the Apron Strings*. Milton Keynes: Open University Press.

Bullough, R.V.J. (1997) 'Becoming a teacher: Self and the social location of teacher education', in B.J. Biddle, T.L. Good and I.F. Goodson (eds) *International Handbook of Teachers and Teaching*. Dordrecht: Kluwer.

Bulmer, M. and Rees, A.M. (eds) (1996) *Citizenship Today*. London: UCL.

Burchall, H. and Millman, V. (eds) (1989) *Changing Perspectives on Gender: New Initiatives in Secondary Education*. Milton Keynes: Open University Press.

Burgess, R.G. (1986) *Sociology, Education and Schools: An Introduction to the Sociology of Education*. London: Batsford.

Burgess, R.G. and Parker, A. (1999) 'Education', in S. Taylor (ed.) *Sociology: Issues and Debates*. London: Macmillan.

Campbell, R.J. and Neill, S.R. St J. (1994) *Curriculum Reform at Key Stage 1 – Teacher Commitment and Policy Failure*. London: Longman.

Cannan, J. and Griffin, C. (1990) 'The new men's studies: Part of the problem or part of the solution?', in J. Hearn and D. Morgan (eds) *Men, Masculinities and Social Theory*. London: Unwin Hyman.

Carr, W. and Kemmis, S. (1986) *Becoming Critical: Education, Knowledge and Action Research*. London: Falmer.

Carrington, B. and Wood, E. (1983) 'Body-talk: Images of sport in a multi-ethnic school', *Multi-Racial Education*, 11(2), 29–38.

Carroll, S. and Walford, G. (1997) 'Parents' responses to the school quasi-market', *Research Papers in Education*, 12(1), 3–26.

Cave, E. and Wilkinson, C. (eds) (1990) *Marketing the School: Local Management of Schools: Some Practical Issues*. London: Routledge.

Chase, S.E. (1995) *Ambiguous Empowerment: The Work Narratives of Women School Superintendents*. Amherst, MA: University of Massachusetts Press.

Chessum, L. (1989) 'A Countesthorpe tale', in C. Harber and R. Meighan (eds) *The Democratic School: Educational Management and the Practice of Democracy*. Derbyshire: Education Now.

Chisholm, L. and Holland, J. (1987) 'Anti-sexist action research in schools: The Girls and Occupational Choice Project', in G. Weiner and M. Arnot (eds) *Gender under Scrutiny*. London: Hutchinson.

Chiswell, K. (1995) 'How is action research helping to develop my role as a communicator?' *British Educational Research Journal*, 21(3), 413–20.

Citizenship Advisory Group (1998) *Report of the Advisory Group on Education for Citizenship and the Teaching of Democracy in Schools*. London: Qualifications and Curriculum Authority.

Clarke, G. (1996) 'Conforming and contesting with (a) difference: How lesbian students and teachers manage their identities', *International Studies in Sociology of Education*, 6(2), 191–210.

Clegg, D. and Billington, S. (1994) *Making the Most of your Inspection*. London: Falmer.

Coates, J. and Cameron, D. (eds) (1989) *Women and Their Speech Communities: New Perspectives on Language and Sex*. London: Longman.

Cody, C.B., Woodward, A. and Elliott, D. (1993) 'Race, ideology and the battle over curriculum', in C. Marshall (ed.) *The New Politics of Race and Gender*. Washington, DC: Falmer.

Coffey, A. (1992) 'Initial teacher education: The rhetoric of equal opportunities', *Journal of Educational Policy*, 7(1), 109–13.

Coffey, A. (1996) 'The power of accounts: Authority and authorship in ethnography', *International Journal of Qualitative Studies in Education*, 9(1), 61–74.

Coffey, A. (1999) *The Ethnographic Self: Fieldwork and the Representation of Identity*. London: Sage.

Coffey, A. and Acker, S. (1991) '"Girlies on the warpath": addressing gender in initial teacher education', *Gender and Education*, 3(3), 249–61.

Coffey, A. and Delamont, S. (2000) *Feminism and the Classroom Teacher: Research, Praxis and Pedagogy*. London: RoutledgeFalmer.

Cohen, L. and Manion, L. (1980) *Research Methods in Education*. London: Croom Helm.

Cohen, M. (1998) '"A habit of healthy idleness": Boys' underachievement in historical perspective', in D. Epstein, J. Elwood, V. Hey and J. Maw (eds) *Failing Boys? Issues in Gender and Achievement*. Buckingham: Open University Press.

Collinson, D. and Hearn, J. (1996) 'Men at "work": Multiple masculinities/multiple workplaces', in M. Mac an Ghaill (ed.) *Understanding Masculinities*. Buckingham: Open University Press.

Coloroso, B. (1982) *Discipline: Winning at Teaching Without Beating Your Kids*. Boulder, CO: Media for Kids.

Commeyras, M. and Alvermann, D.E. (1996) 'Reading about women in world history textbooks from one feminist perspective', *Gender and Education*, 8(1), 31–48.

Commission on Citizenship (1990) *Encouraging Citizenship*. London: HMSO.

Connell, R.W. (1987) *Gender and Power*. Cambridge: Polity Press.

Connell, R.W. (1992) 'Citizenship, social justice and the curriculum', *International Studies in Sociology of Education*, 2(2), 133–46.

Connell, R.W. (1995) *Masculinities*. Cambridge: Polity Press.
Connell, R.W., Ashenden, D.J., Kessler, S. and Dowsett, G.W. (1982) *Making the Difference*. Sydney: Allen & Unwin.
Connelly, F.M. and Clandinin, D.J. (1995) 'Narrative and education', *Teachers and Teaching*, 1(1), 73–86.
Connolly, P. (1995) 'Boys will be boys? Racism, sexuality and the construction of masculinity among infant boys', in J. Holland and M. Blair (eds) *Debates and Issues in Feminist Research and Pedagogy*. Clevedon: Multilingual Matters.
Cortazzi, M. (1991) *Primary Teaching: How It Is*. London: Falmer.
Cotterill, P. and Letherby, G. (1993) 'Weaving stories: Personal auto/biographies in feminist research', *Sociology*, 27(1), 67–80.
Coulby, D. (1991) 'The National Curriculum', in D. Coulby and L. Bash (eds) *Contradiction and Conflict: The 1988 Education Act in Action*. London: Cassell.
Coulby, D. and Bash, L. (eds) (1991) *Contradiction and Conflict: The 1988 Education Act in Action*. London: Cassell.
Croxford, L. (2000) 'Gender and national curricula', in J. Salisbury and S. Riddell (eds) *Gender, Policy and Educational Change*. London: Routledge.
Crozier, G. (1999) 'Parental involvement: Who wants it?' *International Studies in Sociology of Education*, 9(2), 111–30.
Cunnison, S. (1989) 'Gender joking in the staffroom', in S. Acker (ed.) *Teachers, Gender and Careers*. Lewes: Falmer.
David, M. (1993) *Parents, Gender and Education Reform*. Cambridge: Polity Press.
David, M. (1999) 'Home, work, families and children: New Labour, new directions and new dilemmas', *International Studies in Sociology of Education*, 9(3), 209–30.
David, M., West, A. and Ribbens, J. (1994) *Mother's Intuition? Choosing Secondary Schools*. London: Falmer.
Davies, L. (1992) 'School power cultures under economic constraint', *Educational Review*, 43(2), 127–36.
Day, C.W. (1995) 'Qualitative research, professional development and the role of teacher educators: Fitness for purpose', *British Educational Research Journal*, 21(3), 357–70.
Dearing, R. (1994) *The National Curriculum and its Assessment*. London: SCAA.
Dearing, R. (1997) *Report of the National Committee of Inquiry into Higher Education: Higher Education in the Learning Society*. London: HMSO.
Deem, R., Brehony, K. and Heath, S. (1994) 'Governors, schools and the miasma of the market', *British Educational Research Journal*, 20(5), 535–49.
Dei, G.J.S. (1999) 'Knowledge and politics of social change: The implication of anti-racism', *British Journal of Sociology of Education*, 20(3), 395–410.
Dei, G.J.S., Mazzuca, J., McIsaac, E. and Zine, J. (1997) *Reconstructing Drop-out: A Critical Ethnography of the Dynamics of Black Students' Disengagement from School*. Toronto: University of Toronto Press.
Delamont, S. (1998) 'You need the leotard: Revisiting the first PE lesson', *Sport, Education and Society*, 3(1), 5–17.
Delamont, S. (1999) 'Gender and the discourse of derision', *Research Papers in Education*, 14(1), 3–21.
Delamont, S. (2000) 'The anomalous beasts: Hooligans and the sociology of education', *Sociology*, 34(1), 95–111.
Delamont, S., Atkinson, P. and Coffey A. (2000) 'The twilight years: Educational ethnography and the five moments model', *International Journal of Qualitative Studies in Education*, 13(3), 223–38.
Delamont, S. and Galton, M. (1986) *Inside the Secondary Classroom*. London: Routledge and Kegan Paul.

Denscombe, M. (1985) *Classroom Control: A Sociological Perspective*. London: Allen & Unwin.

Denscombe, M. (1994) *Sociology Update 1994*. Leicester: Olympus Press.

Denzin, N.K. (1989) *Interpretive Biography*. Newbury Park, CA: Sage.

Denzin, N.K. (1997) *Interpretive Ethnography: Ethnographic Practice for the 21st Century*. Thousand Oaks, CA: Sage.

DES (1990) *National Curriculum History Working Group Final Report*. London: Department of Education and Science.

DfEE (1997) *Excellence in Schools*. London: HMSO.

DfEE (1998a) *Draft Guidance on Home–School Agreements*. London: Department for Education and Employment.

DfEE (1998b) *Statistics of Education: Teachers, England and Wales 1998*. London: HMSO.

DoE (1993) Circular 17/93 *Schools Requiring Special Measures*. London: Department of Education, Cmnd 2021.

Donald, P., Gosling, S., Hamilton, J. *et al.* (1995) '"No problem here": Action research against racism in a mainly white area', *British Educational Research Journal*, 21(3), 263–76.

Drew, D. and Gray, J. (1991) 'The Black–White gap in examination results: A statistical critique of a decade's research', *New Community*, 17(2), 159–72.

Dwyer, K. (1977) 'On the dialogue of fieldwork', *Dialectical Anthropology*, 2, 143–51.

Easthope, C. and Easthope, G. (2000) 'Intensification, extension and complexity of teachers' workload', *British Journal of Sociology of Education*, 21(1), 43–58.

Edwards, A. (1995) 'Teacher education: Partnerships in pedagogy?' *Teaching and Teacher Education*, 11(6), 595–610.

Edwards, T. (1990) 'Schools of education: Their work and their future', in J.B. Thomas (ed.) *British Universities and Teacher Education: A Century of Change*. Lewes: Falmer.

Edwards, T., Gewirtz, S. and Whitty, G. (1992) 'Whose choice of schools?', in M. Arnot and L. Barton (eds) *Voicing Concerns*. Wallingford: Triangle.

Ehrlich, S. and King, R. (1992) 'Gender based language reform and the social construction of meaning', *Discourse and Society*, 3(2), 151–7.

Elliott, J. (1991) *Action Research for Educational Change*. Buckingham: Open University Press.

Elliott, J. and Sarland, C. (1995) 'A study of "teachers as researchers" in the context of award-bearing courses and research degrees', *British Educational Research Journal*, 21(3), 371–86.

Ellis, C. (1995) *Final Negotiations: A Story of Love, Loss and Chronic Illness*. Philadelphia, PA: Temple University Press.

Ellis, C. and Bochner, A.P. (eds) (1996) *Composing Ethnography: Alternative Forms of Qualitative Writing*. Walnut Creek, CA: Altamira Press.

Ellis, C. and Bochner, A. (2000) 'Autoethnography, personal narrative, reflexivity: Researcher as subject', in N.K. Denzin and Y.S. Lincoln (eds) *Handbook of Qualitative Research*, 2nd edn. Thousand Oaks, CA: Sage.

Ely, M., Vinz, R., Downing, M. and Anzul, M. (1997) *On Writing Qualitative Research: Living by Words*. London: Falmer.

EOC (1989) *Initial Teacher Training in England and Wales*. Manchester: Equal Opportunities Commission.

Epstein, D. (ed.) (1994) *Challenging Lesbian and Gay Inequalites in Education*. Buckingham: Open University Press.

Epstein, D. (1997) 'Boyz own stories: Masculinities and sexualities in schools', *Gender and Education*, 9(1), 105–15.

Epstein, D., Elwood, J., Hey, V. and Maw, J. (eds) (1998) *Failing Boys? Issues in Gender and Achievement*. Buckingham: Open University Press.

Epstein, D. and Johnson, R. (1998) *Schooling Sexualities*. Buckingham: Open University Press.

Erben, M. (1993) 'The problem of other lives: Social perspectives on written biography', *Sociology*, 27(1), 15–26.

Esland, G. (1971) 'Teaching and learning as the organization of knowledge', in M.F.D. Young (ed.) *Knowledge and Control: New Directions for the Sociology of Education*. London: Macmillan.

European Commission (1996) *Teaching and Learning: Towards the Learning Society*. Luxembourg: Office for Official Publications of the European Community.

Evans, K. (1995) 'Competence and citizenship: Towards a complementary model for times of critical social change', *British Journal of Education and Work*, 8(2), 14–27.

Evans, T.D. (1988) *A Gender Agenda: A Sociological Study of Teachers, Parents and Pupils in Their Primary Schools*. Sydney: Allen & Unwin.

Fenwick, D.T. (1998) 'Managing space, energy and self: Junior high school teachers' experiences of classroom management', *Teaching and Teacher Education*, 14(6), 619–32.

Ferfolja, T. (1998) 'Australian lesbian teachers: A reflection of homophobic harassment of high school teachers in New South Wales government schools', *Gender and Education*, 10(4), 401–16.

Fine, M. (1997) '[Ap]parent involvement: Reflections on parents, power and urban public schools', in A.H. Halsey, H. Lauder, P. Brown and A. Stuart Wells (eds) *Education: Culture, Economy, Society*. Oxford: Oxford University Press.

Fisher, G. (1990) 'An insulated island race', *Times Educational Supplement*, 11 May: A18.

Fitz, J., Halpin, D. and Power, S. (1993) *Grant Maintained Schools: Education in the Market Place*. London: Kogan Page.

Flax, J. (1993) 'The age of innocence', in J. Butler and J.W. Scott (eds) *Feminists Theorize the Political*. New York, NY: Routledge.

Fordham, S. (1996) *Blacked Out: Dilemmas of Race, Identity and Success at Capital High*. Chicago, IL: University of Chicago Press.

Foster, P. (1990) *Policy and Practice in Multicultural and Anti-Racist Education*. London: Routledge.

Foster, P. (1992) 'Equal treatment and cultural difference in multi-ethnic schools: A critique of the teacher ethnocentrism theory', *International Studies in Sociology of Education*, 2(1), 89–103.

Foster, P. (1993) 'Some problems in establishing equality of treatment in multi-ethnic schools', *British Journal of Sociology*, 44(3), 519–35.

Foster, P., Gomm, R. and Hammersley, M. (1996) *Constructing Educational Inequality*. London: Falmer.

Foster, P. and Hammersley, M. (1998) 'A review of reviews: Structure and function in reviews of educational research', *British Educational Research Association Journal*, 24(5), 609–28.

Foucault, M. (1974) *The Archeology of Knowledge*. London: Tavistock.

Foucault, M. (1982) 'The subject and power', in H.L. Dreyfus and P. Rabinov (eds) *Michel Foucault: Beyond Structuralism and Hermeneutics*. Brighton: Harvester Wheatsheaf.

Fox-Genovese, E. (1986) 'The claims of a common culture: Gender, race, class and the canon', *Salmagundi*, 72(Fall), 134–51.

France, A. (1996) 'Youth and citizenship in the 1990s', *Youth and Policy*, 53, 28–43.

French, J. and French, P. (1993) 'Gender imbalances in the primary classroom: An interactional account', in P. Woods and M. Hammersley (eds) *Gender and Ethnicity in Schools*. London: Routledge.

Frost, D. (1995) 'Integrating systematic enquiry into everyday professional practice: Towards some principles of procedure', *British Educational Research Journal*, 21(3), 307–22.

Furlong, J., Whitty, G., Miles, S., Barton, L. and Barrett, E. (1996) 'From integration to partnership: Changing structures in ITE', in R. McBride (ed.) *Teacher Education Policy: Some Issues Arising from Research and Practice*. London: Falmer.

Furlong, V.J., Hirst, P.H., Pocklington, K. and Miles, S. (1988) *Initial Teacher Training and the Role of the School*. Milton Keynes: Open University Press.

Gewirtz, S., Ball, S.J. and Bowe, R. (1995) *Markets, Choice and Equity in Education*. Buckingham: Open University Press.

Giddens, A. (1984) *The Constitution of Society*. Cambridge: Polity Press.

Gillborn, D. (1990) *'Race', Ethnicity and Education: Teaching and Learning in Multi-Ethnic Schools*. London: Unwin Hyman/Routledge.

Gillborn, D. (1992) 'Citzenship, "race" and the hidden curriculum', *International Studies in Sociology of Education*, 2(1), 57–73.

Gillborn, D. (1995) *Racism and Antiracism in Real Schools*. Buckingham: Open University Press.

Gillborn, D. (1998) 'Racism and the politics of qualitative research: Learning from controversy and critique', in P. Connolly and B. Troyna (eds) *Researching Racism in Education: Politics, Theory and Practice*. Buckingham: Open University Press.

Gillborn, D. and Drew, D. (1993) 'The politics of research: Some observations on "methodological purity"', *New Community*, 19, 354–60.

Gillborn, D. and Gipps, C. (1996) *Recent Research on the Achievements of Ethnic Minority Pupils*. London: HMSO.

Giroux, H.A. (1988) 'Critical theory and the politics of culture and voice: Rethinking the discourses of educational research', in R.R. Shermann and R.B. Webb (eds) *Qualitative Research in Education: Focus and Methods*. Lewes: Falmer.

Glass, D. (ed.) (1954) *Social Mobility in Britain*. London: Routledge and Kegan Paul.

Glatter, R., Woods, P.A. and Bagley, C. (eds) (1997) *Choice and Diversity in Schooling: Perspectives and Prospects*. London: Routledge.

Glendinning, C. and Millar, J. (eds) (1992) *Women and Poverty in Britain: The 1990s*. London: Harvester Wheatsheaf.

Goffman, E. (1959) *The Presentation of Self in Everyday Life*. New York, NY: Doubleday.

Goldthorpe, J. with Llewellyn, C. and Payne, C. (1980) *Social Mobility and Class Structure in Great Britain*. Cambridge: Cambridge University Press.

Goodlad, J. (1991) *Teachers for our Nation's Schools*. San Francisco, CA: Jossey-Bass.

Goodson, I.F. (1981) 'Life history and the study of sociology', *Interchange*, 11(4), 62–76.

Goodson, I.F. (1988) *The Making of the Curriculum: Collected Essays*. New York, NY: Falmer.

Goodson, I.F. (ed.) (1992) *Studying Teachers' Lives*. London: Routledge.

Goodson, I.F. (1997) 'The life and work of teachers', in B.J. Biddle, T.L. Good and I.F. Goodson (eds) *International Handbook of Teachers and Teaching*. Dordrecht: Kluwer.

Gorard, S. (1997a) *School Choice in an Established Market*. Aldershot: Ashgate.

Gorard, S. (1997b) *Parents, Children and Choice*. Cardiff: School of Education, Cardiff University.

Gorard, S. and Fitz, J. (1998) 'The more things change . . . the missing impact of marketization?', *British Journal of Sociology of Education*, 19(3), 365–76.

Gorard, S., Rees, G. and Salisbury, J. (1999) 'Reappraising the apparent underachievement of boys at school', *Gender and Education*, 11(4), 441–54.

Gordon, T. (1986) *Democracy in One School: Progressive Education and Restructuring*. Lewes: Falmer.

Gordon, T. (1992) 'Citizens and others: Gender, democracy and education', *International Studies in Sociology of Education*, 2(1), 43–56.

Gore, J.M. and Zeichner, K.M. (1991) 'Action research and reflective teaching in preservice teacher education', *Teaching and Teacher Education*, 7, 119–36.

Gosden, P. (1990) 'The James report and recent history', in J.B. Thomas (ed.) *British Universities and Teacher Education: A Century of Change*. Lewes: Falmer.

Graddol, D. and Swann, J. (1989) *Gender Voices*. Oxford: Blackwell.

Gray, J. (1998) 'Telling data: From "A Tale of Inclusion"', *International Journal of Qualitative Studies in Education*, 11(4), 579–81.

Gray, J., Hopkins, D., Reynolds, D. *et al.* (1999) *Improving Schools: Performance and Potential*. Buckingham: Open University Press.

Gray, L. (1992) 'Marketing the school as an educational institution', in N. Foskett (ed.) *Managing External Relations in Schools: A Practical Guide*. London: Routledge.

Gregg, J. (1995) 'Discipline, control and the school mathematics tradition', *Teaching and Teacher Education*, 11(6), 579–94.

Griffin, P. (1991) 'From hiding out to coming out! Empowering lesbian and gay educators', *Journal of Homosexuality*, 2, 167–95.

Hall, S. and Jacques, M. (1989) *New Times*. London: Lawrence and Wishart.

Hall, T., Williamson, H. and Coffey, A. (1998) 'Conceptualizing citizenship: Young people and the transition to adulthood', *Journal of Education Policy*, 13(3), 301–15.

Halsey, A.H., Lauder, H., Brown, P. and Wells, A. Stuart (eds) (1997) *Education: Culture, Economy, Society*. Oxford: Oxford University Press.

Hammersley, M. (1991) *Reading Ethnographic Research: A Critical Guide*. London: Longman.

Hammersley, M. (1993) 'On methodological purism: A response to Barry Troyna', *British Educational Research Journal*, 19(4), 339–41.

Hammersley, M. (1995) *The Politics of Social Research*. London: Sage.

Hammersley, M. and Gomm, R. (1993) 'A response to Gillborn and Drew on "race", class and school effects', *New Community*, 19(2), 348–53.

Hammersley, M. and Gomm, R. (1996) 'Exploiting sociology for equality?', *Network: Newsletter of the British Sociological Association*, 65, 19–20.

Hammond, P.E. (ed.) (1964) *Sociologists at Work: Essays on the Craft of Social Research*. New York, NY: Basic Books.

Hampton, H. (1992) '"One of the small details that got overlooked": school meals as a response to cultural diversity', *Research Papers in Education*, 7(2), 173–94.

Harber, C. and Meighan, R. (eds) (1989) *The Democratic School: Educational Management and the Practice of Democracy*. Derby: Education Now.

Hargreaves, A. (1978) 'Power and the paracurriculum', in C. Richards (ed.) *Power and the Curriculum: Issues in Curriculum Studies*. Driffield: Nafferton.

Hargreaves, A. (1994) *Changing Teachers, Changing Times: Teachers' Work and Culture in the Postmodern Age*. London: Cassell.

Hargreaves, A. and Moore, S. (2000) 'Educational outcomes, modern and postmodern interpretations: Response to Smyth and Dow', *British Journal of Sociology of Education*, 21(1), 27–42.

Hargreaves, D. (1996) Teaching as a research-based profession: possibilities and prospects, Teacher Training Agency annual lecture, University of Cambridge, May.

Harrington, H.L., Quinn-Leering, K. and Hodson, L. (1996) 'Written case analysis and critical reflection', *Teaching and Teacher Education*, 12(1), 25–38.

Harrison, M.L. (1991) 'Citizenship, consumption and rights: A comment on B.S. Turner's theory of citizenship', *Sociology*, 25(2), 209–13.

Hastrup, K. (1992) 'Writing ethnography: State of the art', in J. Okely and H. Callaway (eds) *Anthropology and Autobiography*. London: Routledge.

Hatcher, R. (1998) 'Class differentiation in education: Rational choices?', *British Journal of Sociology of Education*, 19(1), 5–24.

Hatcher, R. and Jones, K. (eds) (1996) *Education after the Conservatives: The Response to the New Agenda of Reform*. Stoke on Trent: Trentham Books.

Haw, K. (with contributions from Shah, S. and Hanifa, M.) (1998) *Educating Muslim Girls: Shifting Discourses*. Buckingham: Open University Press.

Haywood, C. and Mac an Ghaill, M. (1996) 'Schooling masculinities', in M. Mac an Ghaill (ed.) *Understanding Masculinities*. Buckingham: Open University Press.

Hesketh, A.J. and Knight, P. (1998) 'Secondary school prospectuses and educational markets', *Cambridge Journal of Education*, 28, 21–36.

Hexhall, I. and Mahony, P. (1998) 'Effective teachers for effective schools', in R. Slee, G. Weiner with S. Tomlinson (eds) *School Effectiveness for Whom? Challenges to the School Effectiveness and School Improvement Movements*. London: Falmer.

Heywood-Everett, G. (1999) 'The business of learning: Parents as full, unwilling or sleeping partners', *International Studies in Sociology of Education*, 9(2), 159–70.

Hillage, J., Pearson, R., Anderson, A. and Tamkin, P. (1998) *Excellence in Research on Schools*. London: DfEE.

Hills, J. (1995) *Joseph Rowntree Inquiry into Income and Wealth*. York: Joseph Rowntree Foundation.

Hodkinson, H. and Hodkinson, P. (1999) 'Teaching to learn, learning to teach? School based non teaching activity in an initial teacher education and training partnership scheme', *Teaching and Teacher Education*, 15(3), 273–86.

Hoff, J. (1994) 'Gender as a postmodern category of paralysis', *Women's History Review*, 3(2), 149–68.

Holland, J., Ramazanoglu, C., Scott, S., Sharpe, S. and Thomson, R. (1991) *Pressure, Resistance, Empowerment: Young Women and the Negotiation of Safer Sex*. London: Tufnell Press.

Holly, L. (ed.) (1989) *Girls and Sexuality: Teaching and Learning*. Milton Keynes: Open University Press.

Holquist, M. (1990) *Dialogism: Bakhtin and His World*. London: Routledge.

Huberman, M. with Grounauer, M. and Marti, J. (1993) *The Lives of Teachers*. New York, NY: Teachers College Press.

Huberman, M., Thompson, C.L. and Weiland, S. (1997) 'Perspectives on the teaching career', in B.J. Biddle, T.L. Good and I.F. Goodson (eds) *International Handbook of Teachers and Teaching*. Dordrecht: Kluwer.

Hughes, M., Wikely, F. and Nash, T. (1994) *Parents and their Children's Schools*. Oxford: Blackwell.

Jackson, D. (1998) 'Breaking out of the binary trap: Boys' underachievement, schooling and gender relations', in D. Epstein, J. Elwood, V. Hey and J. Maw (eds) *Failing Boys? Issues in Gender and Achievement*. Buckingham: Open University Press.

Jackson, D. and Salisbury, J. (1996) 'Why should secondary schools take working with boys seriously?', *Gender and Education*, 8(1), 103–16.

Jackson, P.W. (1968) *Life in Classrooms*. New York, NY: Holt Rinehart and Winston.

James, P. (1996) 'Learning to reflect: A story of empowerment', *Teaching and Teacher Education*, 12(1), 81–97.

Jeffrey, B. (1999) 'Side-stepping the substantial self: The fragmentation of primary teachers' professionality through audit accountability', in M. Hammersley (ed.) *Researching School Experience: Ethnographic Studies of Teaching and Learning*. London: Falmer.

Jones, C. and Mahony, P. (eds) (1989) *Learning Our Lines: Sexuality and Social Control in Education*. London: The Women's Press.

Jones, G. and Wallace, C. (1992) *Youth, Family and Citizenship*. Buckingham: Open University Press.

Kehily, M.J. (1995) 'Self narration, autobiography and identity construction', *Gender and Education*, 7(1), 23–32.

Kelly, A. (1985) 'Changing schools and changing society: Some reflections on the Girls into Science and Technology project', in M. Arnot (ed.) *Race and Gender: Equal Opportunities Policies in Education*. Oxford: Pergamon.

Kenway, J. (1993) *Economizing Education: The Post-Fordist Directions*. Geelong, Victoria: Deakin University Press.

Kenway, J. (1995) 'Masculinities in schools: Under siege, on the defensive and under reconstruction?', *Discourse*, 16, 59–79.

Kessler, S., Ashenden, D.J., Connell, R.W. and Dowsett, G.W. (1985) 'Gender relations in secondary school', *Sociology of Education*, 58, 34–48.

Khayatt, M.D. (1992) *Lesbian Teachers: An Invisible Presence*. Albany, NY: State University of New York Press.

Khayatt, M.D. (1997) 'Sex and the teacher: Should we come out in class?', *Harvard Educational Review*, 6(7), 126–43.

Klages, M. (1994) 'The ins and outs of a lesbian academic', in L. Garber (ed.) *Tilting the Tower: Lesbians/Teaching/Queer Subject*. New York, NY: Routledge.

Koerner, M.E. (1992) 'Teachers' images: Reflections of themselves', in W.H. Schubert and W.C. Ayers (eds) *Teacher Lore: Learning from Our Own Experience*. New York, NY: Longman.

Kruse, A.M. (1996) 'Approaches to teaching girls and boys: Current debates, practices and perspectives in Denmark', *Women's Studies International Forum*, 19, 429–45.

Lash, S. and Urry, J. (1987) *The End of Organized Capitalism*. Cambridge: Polity Press.

Lather, P. (1991) *Getting Smart: Feminist Research With/In the Postmodern*. London: Routledge.

Le Grand, J. and Bartlett, W. (1993) *Quasi-Markets and Social Policy*. Basingstoke: Macmillan.

Lincoln, Y.S. and Denzin, N.K. (1994) 'The fifth moment', in N.K. Denzin and Y.S. Lincoln (eds) *Handbook of Qualitative Research*. Thousand Oaks, CA: Sage.

Lingard, B. and Douglas, P. (1999) *Men Engaging Feminisms*. Buckingham: Open University Press.

Lister, R. (1997) *Citizenship: Feminist Perspectives*. London: Macmillan.

Lyotard, J.F. (1992) *The Postmodern Condition*. Manchester: Manchester University Press.

Mac an Ghaill, M. (1988) *Young, Gifted and Black: Student–Teacher Relations in the Schooling of Black Youth*. Milton Keynes: Open University Press.

Mac an Ghaill, M. (1994) *The Making of Men: Masculinities, Sexualities and Schooling*. Buckingham: Open University Press.

Mac an Ghaill, M. (ed.) (1996) *Understanding Masculinities*. Buckingham: Open University Press.

McCoy, K. (1997) 'White noise – the sound of epidemic: Reading/writing a climate of intelligibility around the "crisis" of difference', *International Journal of Qualitative Studies in Education*, 10(3), 333–48.

McKeganey, N.P. and Cunningham-Burley, S. (eds) (1987) *Enter the Sociologist: Reflections on the Practice of Sociology*. Aldershot: Avebury.

McKinnon, M. and Ahola-Sidaway, J. (1995) 'Working with the boys: A North American perspective on non-traditional work initiatives for adolescent females in secondary school', *Gender and Education*, 7(3), 327–40.

McLaughlin, H.J. (1991) 'Reconciling caring and control: Authority in classroom relationships', *Journal of Teacher Education*, 42(3), 189–95.

MacLure, M. and Walker, B.M. (2000) 'Disenchanted evenings: The social organization of talk in parent–teacher consultations in UK secondary schools', *British Journal of Sociology of Education*, 21(1), 5–26.

McPherson, G. (1972) *Small Town Teacher*. Cambridge, MA: Harvard University Press.

Maguire, M. (1995) 'Dilemmas in teaching teachers: The tutor's perspective', *Teachers and Teaching*, 1(1), 119–32.

Maguire, M., Ball, S.J. and Macrae, S. (1999) 'Promotion, persuasion and class-taste: Marketing (in) the UK post-compulsory sector', *British Journal of Sociology of Education*, 20(3), 291–308.

Mahony, P. (1997) 'Talking heads: A feminist perspective on public sector reform in teacher education', *Discourse*, 18(1), 87–102.

Mahony, P. (1998) 'Girls will be girls and boys will be first', in D. Epstein, J. Elwood, V. Hey and J. Maw (eds) *Failing Boys? Issues in Gender and Achievement*. Buckingham: Open University Press.

Mahony, P. and Hexhall, I. (1997) 'Sounds of silence: The social justice agenda of the teacher training agency', *International Studies in Sociology of Education*, 7(2), 137–56.

May, N. and Ruddock, J. (1983) *Sex Stereotyping and the Early Years of Schooling*. Norwich: CARE, University of East Anglia.

Measor, L. (1984) 'Gender and the sciences: Pupils' gender based conceptions of school subjects', in M. Hammersley and A. Hargreaves (eds) *Curriculum Practice*. Lewes: Falmer.

Measor, L. and Sikes, P. (1992) *Gender and Schools*. London: Cassell.

Measor, L. and Woods, P. (1994) *Changing Schools: Pupil Perspectives on Transfer to a Comprehensive*. Buckingham: Open University Press.

Middleton, S. (1995) 'Doing feminist educational theory: A post-modernist perspective', *Gender and Education*, 7(1), 87–100.

Mills, M. and Lingard, B. (1997) 'Masculinity politics, myths and boys' schooling', *British Journal of Educational Studies*, 45, 276–92.

Mirza, H.S. (1992) *Young, Black and Female*. London: Routledge.

Moore, R. and Muller, J. (1999) 'The discourse of "voice" and the problem of knowledge and identity in the Sociology of Education', *British Journal of Sociology of Education*, 20(2), 189–206.

Morley, L. and Rassool, N. (1999) *School Effectiveness: Fracturing the Discourse*. London: Falmer.

Morris, K. and Fuller, M. (1999) 'Heterosexual relationships of young women in a rural environment', *British Journal of Sociology of Education*, 20(4), 531–44.

Morrow, V. and Richards, M. (1996) *Transitions to Adulthood: A Family Matter?* York: YPS for the Joseph Rowntree Foundation.

Mortimore, P. and Whitty, G. (1997) *Can School Improvement Overcome the Effects of Disadvantage?* London: Institute of Education.

Mulkay, M.J. (1985) *The Word and the World: Explorations in the Form of Sociological Analysis*. London: Allen & Unwin.

Munro, P. (1998) *Subject to Fiction: Women Teachers' Life History Narratives and the Cultural Politics of Resistance*. Buckingham: Open University Press.

Murphy, R. (1996) 'Like a bridge over troubled water; Realising the potential of educational research', *British Educational Research Journal*, 22(1), 3–16.

Mykhalovskiy, E. (1997) 'Reconsidering "table talk": Critical thoughts on the relationship between sociology, autobiography and self-indulgence', in R. Hertz (ed.) *Reflexivity and Voice*. Thousand Oaks, CA: Sage.

Nance, D. and Fawns, R. (1993) 'Teachers' working knowledge and training: The Australian agenda for reform of teacher education', *Journal of Education for Teaching*, 19(2), 159–73.

Nash, R. (1997) *Inequality/Difference: A Sociology of Education*. Palmerston North: ERDC Press.

Nash, R. (1999) 'Realism in the Sociology of Education: "Explaining" social differentials in attainment', *British Journal of Sociology of Education*, 20(1), 107–25.

NCC (1990) *Curriculum Guidance 8: Education for Citizenship*. York: National Curriculum Council.

Noffke, S.E. and Stevenson, R.B. (eds) (1995) *Educational Action Research: Becoming Practically Critical*. New York: Teachers College Press.

OECD (1995) *Schools under Scrutiny*. Paris: OECD.

Ofsted (1994) *Improving Schools*. London: HMSO.

Ofsted (1995) *The Annual Report of Her Majesty's Chief Inspector of Schools*. London: Ofsted/HMSO.

Ofsted (1996) *Subjects and Standards*. London: Ofsted/HMSO.

Ofsted (1997) *From Failure to Success: How Special Measures Are Helping Schools Improve*. London: HMSO.

Okely, J. and Callaway, H. (eds) (1992) *Anthropology and Autobiography*. London: Routledge.

Ozga, J. (2000) *Policy Research in Educational Settings: Contested Terrain*. Buckingham: Open University Press.

Paechter, C. (1998) *Educating the Other: Gender, Power and Schooling*. London: Falmer.

Paechter, C. and Weiner, G. (1996) 'Editorial', *British Educational Research Journal*, 22(3), 267–71.

Paget, M.A. (1993) *A Complex Sorrow: Reflections on Cancer and an Abbreviated Life*. Philadelphia, PA: Temple University Press.

Parry, O. (1996) 'Cultural contexts and school failure: Underachievement of Caribbean males in Jamaica, Barbados and St Vincent and the Grenadines'. Paper presented to ESRC seminar series 'Gender and Schooling: Are Boys Now Underachieving?', University of London Institute of Education.

Pilkington, A. (1999) 'Racism in schools and ethnic differentials in educational achievement: A brief comment on a recent debate', *British Journal of Sociology of Education*, 20(3), 410–17.

Plummer, K. (1983) *Documents of Life*. London: Allen & Unwin.

Plummer, K. (1995) *Telling Sexual Stories: Power, Change and Social Worlds*. London: Routledge.

Power, S. (1991) ' "Pastoral care" as curriculum discourse: A study in the reformulation of "academic" schooling', *International Studies in Sociology of Education*, 1, 193–208.

Power, S., Whitty, G. and Edwards, T. (1998a) 'Schoolboys and schoolwork: Gender identification and academic achievement', *International Journal of Inclusive Education*, 2(2), 135–53.

Power, S., Whitty, G., Edwards, T. and Wigfall, V. (1998b) 'Schools, families and academically able students: Contrasting modes of involvement in secondary education', *British Journal of Sociology of Education*, 19(2), 157–76.

Proweller, A. (1998) *Constructing Female Identities: Meaning Making in an Upper Middle Class Youth Culture*. Albany, NY: State University of New York Press.

Pugsley, L., Coffey, A. and Delamont, S. (1996) 'Daps, dykes, five mile hikes', *Sport, Education and Society*, 1(2), 133–46.

QAA (1998) *Pilot Studies in Benchmarking Assessment Practice*. Gloucester: Quality Assurance Agency for Higher Education.

QAA (1999) *Code of Practice for the Assurance of Academic Quality and Standards in Higher Education*. Gloucester: Quality Assurance Agency for Higher Education.

Quicke, J. and Winter, C. (1995) 'Best friends: A case study of girls' reactions to an interaction designed to foster collaborative group work', *Gender and Education*, 7(3), 259–82.

Raphael Reed, L. (1998) ' "Zero tolerance": Gender performance and school failure', in D. Epstein, J. Elwood, V. Hey and J. Maw (eds) *Failing Boys? Issues in Gender and Achievement*. Buckingham: Open University Press.

Raphael Reed, L. (1999) 'Troubling boys and disturbing discourses on masculinity and schooling: A feminist exploration of current debates and interventions concerning boys in school', *Gender and Education*, 11(1), 93–110.

Reay, D. (1998) 'Engendering social reproduction: Mothers in the educational market-place', *British Journal of Sociology of Education*, 19(2), 195–210.

Renold, E. (2000) '"Coming out": gender, (hetero)sexuality and the primary school', *Gender and Education*, 12(3), 309–26.

Retana, N. (1998) 'The Hopwood doctorate', *International Journal of Qualitative Studies in Education*, 11(1), 3–4.

Richardson, L. (2000) 'Writing: A method of inquiry', in N.K. Denzin and Y.S. Lincoln (eds) *Handbook of Qualitative Research*, 2nd edition. Thousand Oaks, CA: Sage.

Riseborough, G. (1988) 'Pupils, recipe knowledge, curriculum knowledge and the cultural production of class, ethnicity and patriarchy: A critique of one teacher's practices', *British Journal of Sociology of Education*, 9(1), 39–54.

Roberts, H. (ed.) (1981) *Doing Feminist Research*. London: Routledge and Kegan Paul.

Robertson, S.L. (1999) '"Risky business": Market provision, community governance and the individualization of "risk" in New Zealand education', *International Studies in Sociology of Education*, 9(2), 171–92.

Robinson, K.H. (1992) 'Classroom discipline: Power, resistance and gender', *Gender and Education*, 4(3), 273–87.

Ronai, C.R. (1996) 'My mother is mentally retarded', in C. Ellis and A.P. Bochner (eds) *Composing Ethnography: Alternative Forms of Qualitative Writing*. Walnut Creek, CA: Altamira.

Rust, F. O'Connell (1999) 'Professional conversations: New teachers explore teaching through conversation, story and narrative', *Teaching and Teacher Education*, 15(4), 367–80.

Ryan, C. (1995) 'Initial primary teacher education in a multinational group: A European dimension', *British Educational Research Journal*, 21(3), 289–306.

Sadker, D. and Sadker, M. (1985) 'The treatment of sex equality in teacher education', in S.S. Klein (ed.) *Handbook for Achieving Sex Equality Through Education*. Baltimore, MD: Johns Hopkins University Press.

Salisbury, J. (1996) *Educational Reforms and Gender Equality in Welsh Schools*. Cardiff: Equal Opportunities Commission.

Salisbury, J. and Riddell, S. (eds) (1999) *Gender, Policy and Educational Change: Shifting Agendas in the UK and Europe*. London: Routledge.

Sammons, P., Hillman, J. and Mortimore, P. (1994) *Key Characteristics of Effective Schools: A Review of School Effectiveness*. London: Ofsted.

Schon, D. (1983) *The Reflective Practitioner: How Professionals Think in Action*. New York, NY: Basic Books.

Schon, D. (1987) *Educating the Reflective Practitioner*. San Francisco, CA: Jossey-Bass.

Scott, P. (1989) 'Challenging heterosexism in the curriculum: Roles for teachers, governers and parents', in C. Jones and P. Mahony (eds) *Learning Our Lines: Sexuality and Social Control in Education*. London: The Women's Press.

Sewell, T. (1998) 'Loose cannons: Exploding the myth of the "black macho" lad', in D. Epstein, J. Elwood, V. Hey and J. Maw (eds) *Failing Boys? Issues in Gender and Achievement*. Buckingham: Open University Press.

Shah, S. (1989) 'Effective permeation of race and gender issues in teacher education courses', *Gender and Education*, 1(3), 109–18.

Shakeshaft, C. (1989) *Women in Educational Administration*. Newbury Park, CA: Sage.

Sikes, P., Measor, L. and Woods, P. (1985) *Teacher Careers: Crises and Continuities*. Milton Keynes: Open University Press.

Skelton, C. (1998) 'Feminism and research into masculinities and schooling', *Gender and Education*, 10(2), 217–28.

Slee, R. (1998) 'High reliability organizations and liability students: the politics of reorganization', in R. Slee and G. Weiner, with S. Tomlinson (eds) *School Effectiveness for Whom? Challenges to the School Effectiveness and School Improvement Movements*. London: Falmer.

Slee, R. and Weiner, G. (1998) 'Introduction: school effectiveness for whom?', in R. Slee and G. Weiner, with S. Tomlinson (eds) *School Effectiveness for Whom? Challenges to the School Effectiveness and School Improvement Movements.* London: Falmer.

Slee, R., Weiner, G. with Tomlinson, S. (eds) (1998) *School Effectiveness for Whom? Challenges to the School Effectiveness and School Improvement Movements.* London: Falmer.

Smedley, D. (1995) 'Marketing secondary schools to parents – some lessons from research on parental choice', *Educational Management and Administration*, 23(2), 96–110.

Smith, D., Scott, P. and Lynch, J. (1995) *The Role of Marketing in the University and College Sector.* Leeds: Heist Publications.

Smith, D.J. and Tomlinson, S. (1989) *The School Effect: A Study of Multi-Racial Comprehensives.* London: Policy Studies Institute.

Smith, L.M., Dwyer, D.C., Prunty, J.J. and Kleine, P.F. (1988) *Innovation and Change in Schooling.* New York, NY: Falmer.

Smith, L.M., Prunty, J.J., Dwyer, D.C. and Kleine, P.F. (1987) *The Fate of an Innovative School.* New York, NY: Falmer.

Smyth, J. and Dow, A. (1998) 'What's wrong with outcomes? Spotter planes, action plans and steerage of the educational workplace', *British Journal of Sociology of Education*, 19(3), 291–304.

Somekh, B. (1995) 'The contribution of action research to development in social endeavours: A position paper on action research methodology', *British Educational Research Journal*, 21(3), 339–56.

Southworth, G. and Fielding, M. (1994) 'School inspection for school development?', in G. Southworth (ed.) *Readings in Primary School Development.* London: Falmer.

Sparkes, A.C. (1994) 'Self, silence and invisibility of a beginning teacher: A life history of a lesbian experience', *British Journal of Sociology of Education*, 15(1), 93–118.

Sparkes, A.C. (1995) 'Writing people: Reflections on the dual crises of representation and legitimation in qualitative inquiry', *Quest*, 47(2), 158–95.

Sparkes, A.C., Templin, T.J. and Schempp, P.G. (1990) 'The problematic nature of a career in a marginal subject: Some implications for teacher education', *Journal of Education for Teaching*, 16, 3–28.

Speed, E. (1998) *Gender Issues and Differential Achievement in Educational and Vocational Training: A Research Review.* Manchester: Equal Opportunities Commission.

Spender, D. (1985) *Man-Made Language.* London: Routledge and Kegan Paul.

Spooner, B. (1998) 'A tale of two schools in one city: Foxwood and Cross Green', in R. Slee and G. Weiner, with S. Tomlinson (eds) *School Effectiveness for Whom? Challenges to the School Effectiveness and Improvement Movements.* London: Falmer.

Squirrell, G. (1989) 'In passing . . . teachers and sexual orientation', in S. Acker (ed.) *Teachers, Gender and Careers.* Lewes: Falmer.

Stanley, J. and Wyness, M.G. (1999) 'Living with parental involvement: A case study of two "open schools"', *International Studies in Sociology of Education*, 9(2), 131–58.

Stanley, L. (1990) 'Feminist praxis and the academic mode of production: An editorial introduction', in L. Stanley (ed.) *Feminist Praxis.* London: Routledge.

Stanley, L. (1992) *The Auto/biographical I: Theory and Practice of Feminist Auto/biography.* Manchester: University of Manchester Press.

Stanley, L. (1993) 'On auto/biography in sociology', *Sociology*, 27(1), 41–52.

Stanley, L. and Morgan, D. (1993) 'Editorial introduction', *Sociology*, 27(1), 1–4.

Stanley, L. and Wise, S. (1993) *Breaking Out Again: Feminist Ontology and Epistemology.* London: Routledge.

Stenhouse, L. (1975) *An Introduction to Curriculum Research and Development.* London: Heinemann.

Stolland, L. and Mortimore, P. (1995) *School Effectiveness and School Improvement*. London: University of London Institute of Education.

Stone, L. (1993) 'Contingency: The "constancy of teaching"', *Teachers College Record*, 94(4), 815–35.

Stronach, I. and MacLure, M. (1997) *Educational Research Undone: The Postmodern Embrace*. Buckingham: Open University Press.

Sumison, J. (1999) 'Critical reflections on the experiences of a male early childhood worker', *Gender and Education*, 11(4), 455–68.

Swann, J. and Brown, S. (1997) 'The implementation of a national curriculum and teachers' classroom thinking', *Research Papers in Education*, 12(1), 91–114.

Swann, J. and Graddol, D. (1994) 'Gender inequalities in classroom talk', in D. Graddol, J. Maybin and B. Stierer (eds) *Researching Language and Literacy in Social Context*. Clevedon: Multilingual Matters.

Tartwijk, J. Van, Brekelmans, M., Wubbels, T., Fisher, D.L. and Fraser, B.J. (1998) 'Students' perceptions of teacher interpersonal style: The front of the classroom as the teacher's stage', *Teaching and Teacher Education*, 14(6), 607–18.

Taylor, A. (1995) 'Glass ceilings and stone walls: Employment equity for women in Ontario school boards', *Gender and Education*, 7(2), 123–42.

Teddlie, C. and Reynolds, D. (eds) (1999) *The International Handbook of School Effectiveness Research*. London: Falmer.

Thomas, H. (1979) *History, Capitalism and Freedom*. London: Centre for Policy Studies.

Thorne, B. (1993) *Gender Play: Girls and Boys in School*. New Brunswick, NJ: Rutgers University Press.

Thrupp, M. (1999) *Schools Making a Difference: Let's be Realistic! School Mix, School Effectiveness and the Social Limits of Reform*. Buckingham: Open University Press.

Tillmann-Healy, L.M. (1996) 'A secret life in a culture of thinness: Reflections on body, food and bulimia', in C. Ellis and A.P. Bochner (eds) *Composing Ethnography: Alternative Forms of Qualitative Writing*. Walnut Creek, CA: Altamira.

Todd, E.S. and Higgins, S. (1998) 'Powerlessness in professional and parent partnerships', *British Journal of Sociology of Education*, 19(2), 227–36.

Tomlinson, S. (1997) 'Sociological perspectives on failing schools', *International Studies in Sociology of Education*, 7(1), 81–100.

Tomlinson, S. (1998) A tale of one school in one city: Hackney Downs, in R. Slee, G. Weiner with S. Tomlinson (eds) *School Effectiveness for Whom? Challenges to the School Effectiveness and Improvement Movement*. London: Falmer.

Tooley, J. (1995) *Disestablishing the School*. Aldershot: Avebury.

Tooley, J. (1997) 'On school choice and social class: A response to Ball, Bowe and Gewirtz', *British Journal of Sociology of Education*, 18(2), 217–30.

Tooley, J. (2000) *Reclaiming Education*. London: Cassell.

Tooley, J. and Darby, D. (1998) *Educational Research: A Critique*. London: Office for Standards in Education.

Torrance, H. (1997) 'Assessment, accountability and standards: Using assessment to control the reform of schooling', in A.H. Halsey, H. Lauder, P. Brown and A. Stuart Wells (eds) *Education: Culture, Economy, Society*. Oxford: Oxford University Press.

Torres, C. (1997) 'In memory of Louise Spindler', *International Journal of Qualitative Studies in Education*, 10(4), 499.

Troyna, B. (1993a) *Racism and Education: Research Perspectives*. Buckingham: Open University Press.

Troyna, B. (1993b) 'Underachiever or misunderstood? A reply to Roger Gomm', *British Educational Research Journal*, 19(2), 167–74.

TTA (1996) *A Strategic Plan for Teacher Supply and Recruitment*. London: Teacher Training Agency.

TTA (1998) *National Curriculum for Initial Teacher Training*. London: Teacher Training Agency.

Turner, B.S. (1990) 'Outline of a theory of citizenship', *Sociology*, 24(2), 189–217.

Turner, E., Riddell, S. and Brown, S. (1995) *Gender Equality in Scottish Schools: The Impact of Recent Educational Reforms*. Glasgow: Equal Opportunities Commission.

Usher, R. and Edwards, R. (1994) *Postmodernism and Education*. London: Routledge.

Valli, L. (1992) *Reflective Teaching Education: Cases and Critiques*. Albany, NY: State University of New York Press.

Van Maanen, J. (1988) *Tales of the Field*. Chicago, IL: University of Chicago Press.

Vincent, C. (1996) *Parents and Teachers: Power and Participation*. London: Falmer.

Wade, R.C. and Yarborough, D.B. (1996) 'Portfolios: A tool for reflective thinking in teacher education', *Teaching and Teacher Education*, 12(1), 63–79.

Walford, G. (1994) *Choice and Equity in Education*. London: Cassell.

Walford, G. and Miller, H. (1991) *City Technology Colleges*. Buckingham: Open University Press.

Walkerdine, V. (1988) *The Mastery of Reason: Cognitive Development and the Production of Rationality*. London and New York, NY: Routledge.

Walkerdine, V. (and the Girls and Mathematics Unit) (1989) *Counting Girls Out*. London: Virago.

Waslander, S. and Thrupp, M. (1995) 'Choice, competition and segregation: An empirical analysis of a New Zealand secondary school market 1990–1993', *Journal of Education Policy*, 10, 1–26.

Waslander, S. and Thrupp, M. (1997) 'Choice, competition and segregation: An empirical analysis of a New Zealand secondary school market, 1990–93', in A.H. Halsey, H. Lauder, P. Brown and A. Stuart Wells (eds) *Education: Culture, Economy, Society*. Oxford: Oxford University Press.

Webb, R. and Vulliamy, G. (1996) *Roles and Responsibilities in the Primary School*. Buckingham: Open University Press.

Webb, R., Vulliamy, G., Häkkinen, K. and Hämäläinen, S. (1998) 'External inspection or school self-evaluation? A comparative analysis of policy and practice in primary schools in England and Finland', *British Educational Research Journal*, 24(5), 539–56.

Weiler, K. and Middleton, S. (eds) (1999) *Telling Women's Lives: Narrative Inquiries in the History of Women's Education*. Buckingham: Open University Press.

Weiner, G. (ed.) (1985) *Just a Bunch of Girls: Feminist Approaches to Schooling*. Milton Keynes: Open University Press.

Weiner, G. (1993) 'Shell-shocked or sisterhood: English school history and feminist practice', in M. Arnot and K. Weiler (eds) *Feminism and Social Justice in Education*. London: Falmer.

Weiner, G. (1994) *Feminisms in Education*. Buckingham: Open University Press.

Weiner, G. (1998) 'Review of I. Stronach and M. MacLure (1997) *Educational Research Undone*', *Gender and Education*, 10(4), 461–2.

Weis, L. (1990) *Working Class Without Work*. New York, NY: Routledge.

Welland, T. (1998) ' "Sleeping on the sofa": preparation for ordained ministry and the "curriculum of the body" ', in J. Richardson and A. Shaw (eds) *The Body in Qualitative Research*. Aldershot: Ashgate.

White, J. and Barber, M. (eds) (1997) *Perspectives on School Effectiveness and Improvement*. London: University of London Institute of Education.

Whitehead, J., Menter, I. and Stainton, R. (1996) 'The reform of initial teacher training: The fragility of the new school-based approach and questions of quality', *Research Papers in Education*, 11(3), 307–22.

Whitehead, S. (1998) 'Disrupted selves: Resistance and identity work in the managerial arena', *Gender and Education*, 10(2), 199–215.

Whitty, G. (1997) 'Marketization, the State and the re-formation of the teaching profession', in A.H. Halsey, H. Lauder, P. Brown and A. Stuart Wells (eds) *Education: Culture, Economy, Society*. Oxford: Oxford University Press.

Whyte, J. (1986) *Girls into Science and Technology: The Story of a Project*. London: Routledge and Kegan Paul.

Whyte, J. (1987) 'Issues and dilemmas in action research', in G. Walford (ed.) *Doing Sociology of Education*. London: Falmer.

Wilcox, B. and Gray, J. (1998) *Inspecting Schools: Holding Schools to Account and Helping Schools to Improve*. Buckingham: Open University Press.

Willis, P. (1977) *Learning to Labour*. Aldershot: Gower.

Wolf, M. (1992) *A Thrice Told Tale: Feminism, Postmodernism and Ethnographic Responsibility*. Stanford, CA: Stanford University Press.

Wolf, M. (1996) 'Afterword: Musings from an old gray wolf', in D.L. Wolf (ed.) *Feminist Dilemmas in Fieldwork*. Boulder, CO: Westview.

Woodhead, C. (1998) 'Academia gone to seed', *New Statesman*, 20 March, 51–2.

Woods, P. (1990) *Teacher Skills and Strategies*. London: Routledge.

Woods, P. and Jeffrey, J. (1998) 'Choosing positions: Living the contradictions of Ofsted', *British Journal of Sociology of Education*, 19(4), 547–70.

Woods, P.A., Bagley, C. and Glatter, R. (1998) *School Choice and Competition: Markets in the Public Interest?* London: Routledge.

Wright, C. (1986) 'School processes: An ethnographic study', in J. Eggleston, D. Dunn and M. Anjali (eds) *Education for Some*. Stoke-on-Trent: Trentham Books.

Wright, C. (1992) *Race Relations in the Primary School*. London: David Fulton.

Wright, J. (1998) 'Lesbian instructor comes out: The personal is pedagogy', in G.E. Cohee, E. Daumer, T.D. Kemp *et al.* (eds) *The Feminist Teacher Anthology*. New York, NY: Teachers College Press.

Wright, N. (1983) 'Standards and the Black Papers', in B. Cosin and M. Hales (eds) *Education, Policy and Society*. London: Routledge and Kegan Paul in association with The Open University.

Wylie, C. (1994) *Self Managing Schools in New Zealand*. Wellington: New Zealand Council for Educational Research.

Young, M.F.D. (ed.) (1971) *Knowledge and Control: New Directions for the Sociology of Education*. London: Macmillan.

Zeichner, K.M. and Liston, D.P. (1987) 'Teaching students to reflect', *Harvard Educational Review*, 57, 23–48.

Index

CLASS ANALYSIS AND SOCIAL TRANSFORMATION

Mike Savage

... a tour de force. The style is engaging, quite an achievement for such a complex analysis.

Professor Steve Edgell, University of Salford

- Do we now live in a classless society?
- How is it possible for us to live in a more class-divided society when people's awareness of class is relatively weak?
- What implications do contemporary social and cultural transformations have for understanding the relevance of social class?

Academic discussions about social class tend to be increasingly specialized and have found it difficult to unpack processes of cultural as well as social change. This book breathes new life into class analysis by showing how contemporary social and cultural transformations are related to the restructuring of class relations. Using the British experience as a case study, Mike Savage gives a definitive account of debates on class and finds evidence of both the breaking down and persistence of class divisions. He employs a variety of disciplinary perspectives to provide a comprehensive account of the main features of contemporary social change. Particular attention is paid to arguments developed by Beck and Giddens concerning individualization, and he shows how the redrawing of individual relations is tied in to the remaking of social class in complex and largely unrecognized ways. *Class Analysis and Social Transformation* brings together recent empirical research on class with topical theoretical debates on social and cultural change. It offers a compelling interpretation of the field in its entirety and an authoritative and accessible text for social science students wishing to learn about the debates on class analysis.

Contents

Part I: Issues in class analysis – The travails of class theory – The limits to class consciousness – Economic inequality and social class – Social mobility and the 'Nuffield paradigm' – Part II: New directions in class analysis – Individualization and cultural distinction – The organizational restructuring of class relations – Conclusions: class formation and social change – Bibliography – Index.

208pp   0 335 19327 7 (Paperback)   0 335 19328 5 (Hardback)

DECONSTRUCTING SPECIAL EDUCATION AND CONSTRUCTING INCLUSION

Gary Thomas and Andrew Loxley

Deconstrucing Special Education and Constructing Inclusion is a sophisticated, multidisciplinary critique of special education that leaves virtually no intellectural stone unturned. It is a must read for anyone interested in the role and significance of inclusive pedagogy in the new struggle for an inclusive society.

Professor Tom Skrtic, University of Kansas

In this book the authors look behind special education to its supposed intellectual foundations. They find a knowledge jumble constructed of bits and pieces from Piagetian, psychoanalytic, psychometric and behavioural theoretical models. They examine the consequences of these models' influence for professional and popular thinking about learning difficulty. In turn, they explore and critique the results of this dominance for our views about children who are different and for the development of special education and its associated professions. In the light of this critique, they suggest that much of the 'knowledge' of special education is misconceived, and they proceed to advance a powerful rationale for inclusion out of ideas about stakeholding, social justice and human rights. Concluding that inclusion owes more to political theory than to psychology or sociology, the authors suggest that a rethink is needed about the ways in which we come by educational knowledge. This is important reading for students of education, and for teachers, advisers and educational psychologists.

Contents

Special education: theory and theory talk – The knowledge-roots of special education – The great problem of 'need': a case study in children who don't behave – Thinking about learning failure, especially in reading – Modelling difference – Inclusive schools in an inclusive society? Policy, politics and paradox – Constructing inclusion – References – Index.

160pp   0 335 20448 1 (Paperback)   0 335 20449 X (Hardback)